P9-CAA-683

D0015120

THE ROCKER

The Rocker

AN AMERICAN DESIGN TRADITION

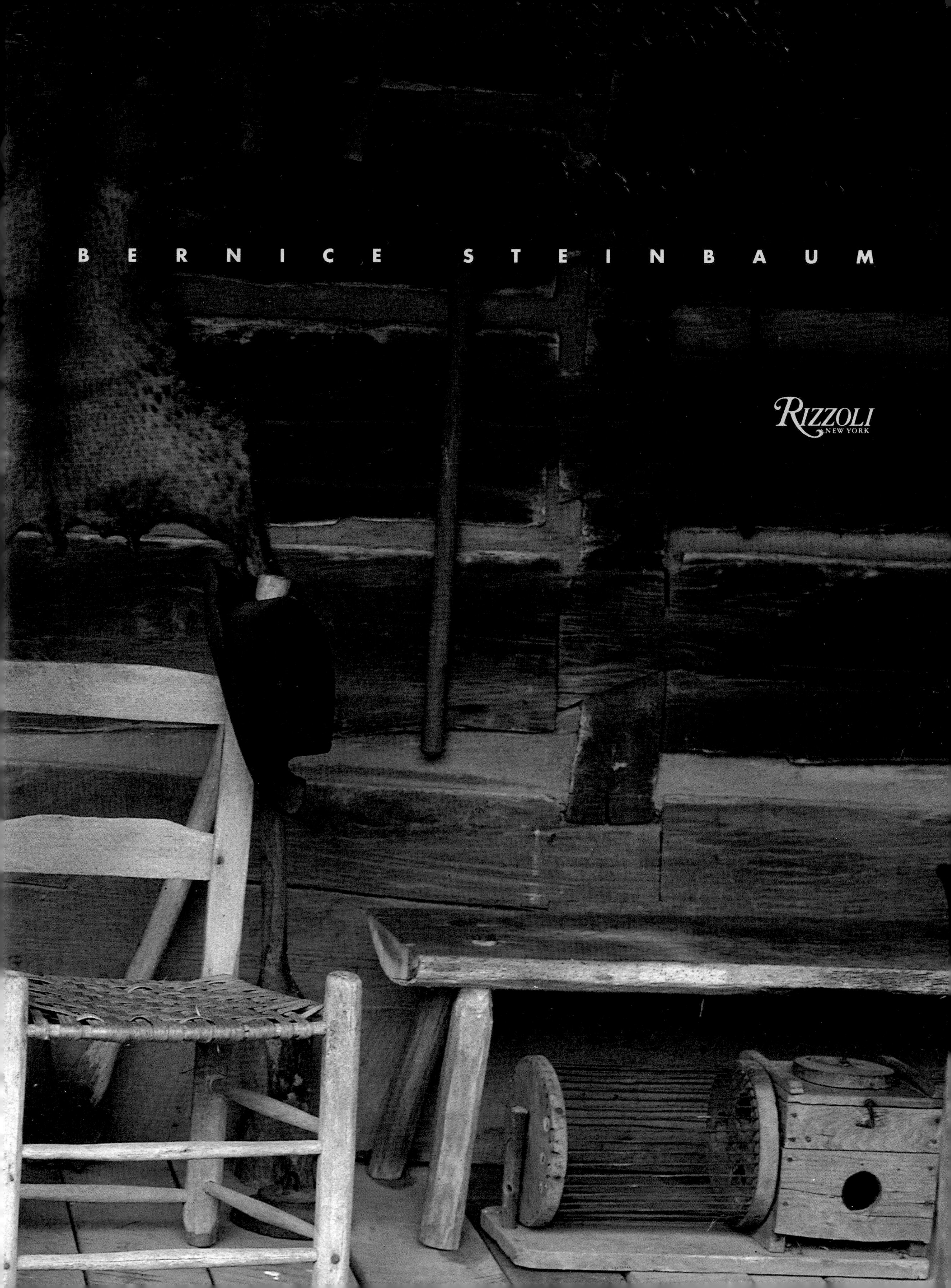

BERNICE STEINBAUM

RIZZOLI
NEW YORK

FIRST PUBLISHED IN
THE UNITED STATES OF AMERICA
IN 1992 BY RIZZOLI INTERNATIONAL
PUBLICATIONS, INC.
300 PARK AVENUE SOUTH
NEW YORK, NEW YORK 10010

COPYRIGHT © BERNICE STEINBAUM

ALL RIGHTS RESERVED.
NO PART OF THIS PUBLICATION MAY BE
REPRODUCED IN ANY MANNER
WHATSOEVER WITHOUT PERMISSION IN
WRITING FROM RIZZOLI INTERNATIONAL
PUBLICATIONS, INC.

LIBRARY OF CONGRESS
CATALOGUING-IN-PUBLICATION DATA
STEINBAUM, BERNICE.
THE ROCKER : AN AMERICAN DESIGN
TRADITION / BERNICE STEINBAUM.
INCLUDES BIBLIOGRAPHICAL REFERENCES
AND INDEX.
ISBN 0-8478-1587-0
1. ROCKING CHAIRS—UNITED STATES—
HISTORY. I. TITLE.
NK2715.S82   1992
749'.32'0973—DC20   92-15145
                              CIP
DESIGNED BY BETH TONDREAU DESIGN
PRINTED AND BOUND IN HONG KONG

PAGE 1: YURI DOJC, THE IMAGE BANK
PAGES 2–3: CHRIS MEAD
PAGES 4–5: CHRIS MEAD
PAGES 6–7: GERHARD GSCHEIDL,
THE IMAGE BANK

CONTENTS

American folklore attributes the rocking chair—as well as the discovery of electricity—to the eccentric inventor and statesman, Benjamin Franklin. While the rocker was probably first invented by an unknown European farmer, it was taken up in America, late in the eighteenth century, like nowhere else in the world.

For over two hundred years, Americans from all walks of life have been rocking, dozing, reading, spinning tall tales, nursing, dreaming, and orating in rocking chairs. The rocking chair—much like Benjamin Franklin—is a homespun symbol of American inventiveness based on practicality and comfort. While the rocker is not necessarily American in origin, like cowboys, who also roam the plains of Argentina, and hotdogs, which certainly came originally from Germany—it is an emblem that Americans have embraced as their own.

The rocker was, most likely, the invention of the English, who were the first to apply skates to ordinary chairs. Yet the invention was not greeted with great enthusiasm. During the Victorian era, in particular, the rocker was frowned upon by polite society who could not understand the colonial fascination with it. The urban English found it cumbersome and declassé.

Despite this, however, the chair found its way into the hearts of Americans and has become a staple in the poorest household as well as the White House. Its popularity is a tribute to native artisans, who were able to transform a borrowed form to suit the needs and tastes of their own people. Not long after the idea took root in America, rockers with rawhide seats were found on Western ranches, in white wicker on Southern porches, lavishly gilded in New England parlors, and in rough-hewn wood or twigs in Appalachia. The rocker was used by slaves, prosperous landowners, Native Americans, the working

OPPOSITE: *Gail Fredell's steel rocker,* Graphite to Taste, *in a Los Angeles loft. (David Wakely)*

LEFT: *Rawhide-seated rockers and chairs. (Chris Mead)*

BELOW: *A mother and child on a tombstone in Newman, Georgia. (Lucinda Bunnen & Virginia Warren Smith)*

RIGHT: *Rockers overlooking the Catskills at Mohonk Mountain House, New Paltz, New York. (Alfred Gescheidt, The Image Bank)*

classes, and countless presidents. John F. Kennedy conducted American foreign policy from a rocker that he had installed in the Oval Office and numerous rural story tellers have preserved the oral histories of their families by telling stories while rocking upon porches. It was and remains today a democratic piece of furniture that transcends economic boundaries.

The American rocker is connected, in many minds, to feelings of family. Early furnituremakers designed rocking chairs specifically for mothers to rock in as they nursed their children, elegant armless "sewing" rockers for women to sit gracefully upon while working, and the "mammy bench"—a charming contraption that allowed a child to be rocked to sleep without danger of falling off the chair. Women, as well, played an active role in actually making, decorating, and caning rocking chairs, particularly among Shaker communities.

While the first rockers were made in Europe, they are rarely seen there today, except occasionally in rural, northern European villages. In America, however, the rocker is thriving. It would be wrong of us to look upon the rocker with nostalgia as simply a piece of Americana, for it continues to fulfill needs today. There is even a Boston doctor who prescribes rockers for patients as an important part of convalescence. Today, the traditional rocker, handed down from generation to generation, offers a link with the past—and, as you will see in the last section of this book—a forum for creatively reinterpreting that past and, perhaps, shaping our future.

OPPOSITE: *Rocker on a porch in a South Carolina mill town. (Peter Bellamy)*

Americans and their Rockers

Since the rocking chair was introduced to this country some two hundred years ago, Americans from all walks of life have incorporated rockers into their lives. **BELOW**, an old Kentucky couple watch the rain from their porch; **OPPOSITE**, Robert Frost on a lawn in New England. *(Arthur Tress, Magnum Photos, Inc.; Burt Glinn, Magnum Photos, Inc.)*

OPPOSITE, Grandma Moses talks with her great grandchildren before a field of corn in Eagle Bridge, New York; BELOW, on a postcard from early in this century, a woman sits with her dog on a press-back rocker; Jimmy Dean rocks while on the phone; and the writer M.F.K. Fisher reads surrounded by her collection of paintings (*Cornell Capa, Magnum Photos, Inc.; Schomburg Center for Research in Black Culture, New York Public Library, Astor, Lenox, and Tilden Foundations; Dennis Stock, Magnum Photos, Inc.; Paul Fusco, Magnum Photos, Inc.*)

Presidential Rockers

Abraham Lincoln's rocker (**TOP LEFT**) is, perhaps, the most infamous of rockers—the president was sitting in it when he was assasinated in Ford's Theater on April 14, 1865. This style of rocker, with comfortable padding, grecian volutes at the arms, and sabre legs has become known as a "Lincoln rocker." Rockers were clearly a part of the lives of many presidents; **BELOW** is the Quincy, Massachusetts, homestead of John Adams with a comb-back Windsor and ladder-back rockers; McKinley at his Ohio farm in 1901 with an Amish-style rocker; Teddy Roosevelt reading and rocking; Lincoln rockers in the nursery of FDR's New York home; Grace and Calvin Coolidge before a rustic

rocker in Vermont, 1961; Eisenhower with his wife and granddaughter in a Boston rocker; and Kennedy in the Oval Office. *(Henry Ford Museum & Greenfield Village, Dearborn, Michigan; Library of Congress; Theodore Roosevelt Collection, Harvard College Library; Library of Congress; Library of Congress; Burt Glinn, Magnum Photos, Inc; AP/Wide World Photos)*

PREVIOUS PAGES.

18-19: *Room in a Pennsylvania country inn, with a ladder-back rocker, Brandywine Valley. (Michael Melford, The Image Bank)*

20-21: *A row of well-worn rockers, Columbia, South Carolina. (Peter Bellamy)*

OPPOSITE: *Hand-tinted photograph of rockers in Uniontown, Alabama. (Virginia Warren Smith)*

THE ROCKER

RIGHT: *Pennsylvania German child's rocker from about 1800, made of poplar, maple, and hickory; the shape of these skates are identical to those used on cradles. (Philadelphia Museum of Art, Gift of Mrs. William D. Frishmuth)*

BELOW: *This Windsor from the Connecticut River Valley shows how rockers were first made in America; skates were simply attached to the legs of ordinary chairs. (Historic Deerfield, Inc., Deerfield, Massachusetts, Amanda Merullo)*

The rocking cradle was in use for centuries before anyone thought to apply the same rocking motion to chairs. Even the invention of the rocking horse probably pre-dated the rocking chair. In America, at least, the earliest docum-entation for a rocker is found in the records of a Massachusetts furnituremaker from the 1760s.

Although no doubt countless experimentations had preceded the work of this colonial furnituremaker, from this point on, the rocking chair entered the daily lives of Americans—and has never left. The first rockers made in this country were simply chairs with skates clumsily bolted onto their legs. Such early converted rockers are quite easy to detect, as can be seen on the chair opposite. The legs, too, would have been fairly straight; whereas chairs made later specifically as rocking chairs rocked on splayed legs. The size of the skate is also a give-away; the first rockers had only small skates, with just a short piece jutting out at the front and back; but later rocker manufacturers extended the back of the skate to provide better stability.

From these first awkward attempts, however, American furnituremakers soon became quite adept with their new chair form, borrowing and adapting European designs. Chair designs and decorations became more and more fanciful. The English Windsor was transformed into an elaborately gilded and stenciled "fancy" chair. The Boston rocker, which was a larger, more ornate version of the Windsor, took over in popularity until the advent of the platform rocker—which succeeded in reviving even European interest in the rocking chair. With its mechanized platform, the homey, hand-crafted image of the American rocking chair had now become a rocking machine for an industrialized country. These rocking chairs reflected the range of tastes of a young country and they are today highly prized artifacts of our early history.

LEFT AND BELOW: *Cradles were used for centuries before the rocker appeared; but the transitional stage, between cradle and rocking chair, is clear from this eighteenth-century Pennsylvania German heart-motif cradle and child's commode chair. The rope webbing seen here was used for cradles, as well as adult beds, to provide a flexible support beneath the mattress; a sash could be attached to the knobs at the side of the crib, to secure a child safely inside. (Philadelphia Museum of Art; the commode is from the Titus C. Geesey Collection, the cradle a Gift of J. Stogdell Stokes)*

ABOVE AND RIGHT: *Rocking horses, too, evolved from the idea of the cradle. (Chris Mead)*

Windsor Rockers

The Windsor chair design originated in England in a small town in Buckinghamshire. It came to prominence, according to legend, in the seventeenth century when King George II, masquerading as a commoner, visited a farmer's cottage in the town of Windsor; he was so taken with the simple spindle-back chairs he found there, that he brought the design back to his own cabinetmakers and had the chair copied for his palace.

By the eighteenth century, Windsors had made their way across the Atlantic to the colonies, and soon, Philadelphia furnituremakers caught on to the vogue and began making Windsors themselves, adapting them to American tastes. The Windsor was turning up in schoolrooms, church pews, as well as the home. Sev-

eral different types of wood were employed in their manufacturing, a softwood, such as pine, for the saddle seat and back and harder woods for the legs. To hide the various grains and wood colors, American Windsors were often painted. Dark green was a favorite, although Benjamin Franklin ordered two dozen in white and Thomas Jefferson commissioned black and gold ones for Monticello. Distinctive styles soon emerged too, from the traditional hoop-back to the birdcage, arrow-back, and the comb-back—considered the most elegant of all.

It was not long before skates were attached to Windsors, shifting them from the dining room and tavern hall to the porch and living room. Gradually, Windsors were made directly—rather than converted after the fact—into rocking chairs, cradles, and rocking benches, including the "mammy" rocker, which enabled a mother to rock her child without using her arms, thus allowing her to read or work with her hands.

The Windsor's popularity continued on into the nineteenth century, growing more and more elaborate with stenciled patterns and gold trimmings, as the fad for "fancy" chairs gained momentum. Early in the nineteenth century, attention shifted from the Windsor to its offspring, the Boston and Salem rockers, made with similarly elegant spindle-backs, but more elaborate seats and crestrails; the Boston rocker, in particular, reigned for the next few decades of the nineteenth century.

OPPOSITE TOP: *A traditional bow- or hoop-back Windsor rocker, c. 1800, made for a child. (Old Sturbridge Village, Sturbridge, Massachusetts, Henry E. Peach)*

OPPOSITE BOTTOM: *A rocking Windsor settee from New England, 1825–75; this type of bench, known as a mammy bench, was fitted with a rail so that a mother could safely rock her child, without danger of it falling. (Historic Deerfield, Inc., Deerfield, Massachusetts, Amanda Merullo)*

TOP LEFT AND RIGHT: *Comb-back and birdcage Windsors, c. 1820–40. (Old Sturbridge Village, Sturbridge, Massachusetts, Henry E. Peach)*

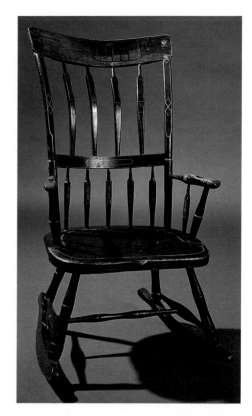

OPPOSITE: *Rocking settee in the Hall Tavern Supper Room at Historic Deerfield; the two portraits are by Ruth Henshaw Bascomb from about 1810; the man is Bascomb's husband Ezekial, the woman is unknown.*
(Amanda Merullo)

ABOVE: *Three Windsor variations; at top left is a mid-nineteenth-century painted comb-back from New Hampshire. It displays the three painting techniques frequently applied to furniture at the time: sponging on the skates, stenciling on the back rails, and grain-painting on the seat. The arrow-back rocker at top right is named for the shape of its flattened, tapering spindles. And bottom right, a yellow-painted chair, c. 1830, in the Windsor style, although also displaying characteristics of the Salem and Boston-style rockers that grew out of the traditional Windsor. (Top left and bottom, Shelburne Museum, Shelburne, Vermont, Ken Burris; top right, Old Sturbridge Village, Sturbridge, Massachusetts, Henry E. Peach)*

Even though the Boston rocker is distinguished as the first widely produced chair and is, perhaps, today the most recognizable of all rocking chairs, its origins remain unclear. What is known is that the Boston rocker developed about 1825, and flourished until the end of the nineteenth century. It is believed to have evolved in Connecticut, rather than Massachusetts, from the Windsor design.

Although many prominent furniture manufacturers incorporated this style into their inventories and catalogues, none ever laid claim to originating the design.

HITCHCOCK BOSTON ROCKER AND DETAIL OF CRESTRAIL MANUFACTURED IN RIVERTON, CONNECTICUT, BETWEEN 1832 AND 1843. ON THE BACK OF THE CRESTRAIL IS STENCILED: HITCHCOCK, ALFORD & CO./ HITCHCOCKS-VILLE, CT. WARRANTED. (THE HITCHCOCK MUSEUM, RIVERTON, CONNECTICUT)

LAMBERT HITCHCOCK

In the first quarter of the nineteenth century, elaborately painted, stenciled, and japanned—or "fancy"—chairs became all the rage; Lambert Hitchcock, a Connecticut chair manufacturer, was largely responsible for popularizing this type of furniture. As a young man, Hitchcock was apprenticed to a cabinetmaker. When he had learned the trade, he opened, in 1826, a factory in Riverton, Connecticut, which came to be known as Hitchcocksville.

Producing only chairs, his small factory thrived; it outfitted churches with finely made and ornamented pews, benches for schoolhouses, and rockers—or "rocky" chairs, as Hitchcock called them, for hearths and porches. The firm may even have been the first to produce the Boston rocker. The chair designs were essentially the same, but there was great variety in the decorating, which was applied by women with stencils and steady hands. The demand for his chairs became so great that Hitchcock had to hire inmates from the local prison to help with the assembling. While he was an excellent salesman, and traveled as far as Chicago by horse to sell his goods, Hitchcock was no businessman. Despite its tremendous success, the finances of the factory were not properly monitored and in 1829, Hitchcock was forced to declare bankruptcy.

Not long after his financial ruin, Hitchcock married Eunice Alford and within a year or two, he formed a partnership with Eunice's brother, Arba Alford, and they opened a new factory. Chairs manufactured during the partnership, such as the rocker shown here, bore the names of both Hitchcock and Alford. This factory, too, was forced to close until 1946, when the Hitchcock Chair Company, which carries on the works of the great chairmaker today, was formed.

RIGHT: *A Pennsylvania German child's rocker from about 1850; the seat, which curves up in the back and down at the front, is the most typical feature of the Boston rocker; originally, as here, the curves of the seat were formed from three separate pieces of wood. Although known as Boston rockers, they were made throughout the country. (Philadelphia Museum of Art, Titus C. Geesey Collection)*

Lambert Hitchcock of Hitchcocksville, Connecticut, for example, one of the best known manufacturers of "fancy" chairs—as the elaborately painted and stenciled furniture popular at the time came to be known—produced a model of the Boston rocker early in the nineteenth century.

The back of the Boston rocker has a similar spindle design to the Windsor, usually two stiles with seven spindles attached between them. (Variations in the number of spindles did occur, and some featured back splats.) It was not unusual for the back spindles to form a curve, to accommodate the back and head of the sitter. At the top of the spindles is the crest, generally a flat horizontal plank linking the two stiles, which many times is decorated with scrolled sides often stenciled with an elaborate design. The spindles and the crest give the chair a distinctive "lyre-like" look.

Traditional in its use of skates or rockers, the Boston rocker remains unique in many ways. Perhaps its most distinctive feature is its curved seat, usually of plank design, which rolls up at the back and down at the front. (The rocker was made primarily of maple, though pine was often used to achieve the roll in the seat.)

In addition to a sloped back and front, the legs of the chair are turned and "raked"—that is, the bottoms of the legs are angled slightly outward in relation to the seat. The skates themselves are normally flat and attached to the legs with wooden dowels. The arms slope gently, mimicking the curve of the seat, and have curved ends which accommodate the palms of the hands. The "Little Boston" rocker was a version without armrests, considered a woman's chair for use while sewing or nursing. The Salem rocker is very similar to the Boston, although some-

BELOW: *A style of rocker with curved seat but no armrests was known as a "Little Boston" rocker and appeared around 1850; the Little Bostons were considered to be made for women as either nursing or sewing chairs. (Nadine Gordon)*

ABOVE: *A typical Boston-style rocker with scrolled back and S-shaped seat on a Victorian porch. (Kaz Mori, The Image Bank)*

OPPOSITE: *Salem-style and ladder-back rockers in an old Maine tavern, Machias. (Paul Rocheleau)*

what lighter in appearance and lacking the characteristic front and back rolling seat of the Boston style; the Pittsburgh rocker is a version of the Boston that incorporates a back splat, flaring crest rail, and scrolled arms.

The stenciled crest lent the Boston rocker caché and certified it as "fancy" furniture, suitable for use in the parlor. As a general rule, the more elaborate the design, the higher the value of the chair. The majority of the designs were of traditional New England motifs, including leaves, flowers, and clumps of fruit. (Many also depicted landscapes, historical scenes, and patriotic figures if the size of the rail allowed.)

After 1840, the majority of Boston rockers were assembled by machine. But the popularity of the style can be gauged by the fact that during the Victorian era most Americans tended to refer to all rocking chairs as Boston rockers. At the onset of the twentieth century, however, the popularity of the Boston rocker began to wane considerably, owing, it seems, to the cumbersome size of its skate construction. This fall coincided with the rise of the patented platform rocker, which was invented and began to flourish in the late 1870s. A common complaint against traditional rockers was that the skates were clumsy and prevented the owner from shoving the chair near a wall and out of the way. The platform rocker,

RIGHT: *Unlike many of the so-called Boston rockers, this one was actually made in the city of Boston, c. 1835. The bronze rosettes painted on the scrolls of the crest rail characterize this as one of the earlier Boston rockers; later gilding was much more elaborate. (Henry Ford Museum & Greenfield Village, Dearborn, Michigan)*

LEFT: *This enormous rocker, six feet high and four feet wide, stood on the roof of the Boston Rocker Factory in Morrisville, Vermont, as the company's trade sign. The date of manufacture, 1849, is painted on the crest rail. (Shelburne Museum, Shelburne, Vermont, Ken Burris)*

in which a spring base or platform was substituted for skates, alleviated this problem and provided noiseless motion without the threat of tipping over or overly aggressive rocking. Later models also incorporated lavish structural ornaments and elegant fabrics and tapestries for seat and back which tended to overshadow the simple stencil designs of the Boston.

Finally, the Boston had become such a familiar chair that it seemed to lack luster for post-Industrial Revolutionary Americans, who were always looking for the new and innovative. Nevertheless, it has remained a cherished piece of American fancy furniture.

LEFT: *The larger tablet at the back of Boston and Salem rockers allowed painters to move away from the traditional fruit and leaf motifs to paint such lively scenes as this little pastoral. (Henry Ford Museum & Greenfield Village, Dearborn, Michigan)*

FOLLOWING: *Various rocker styles on the porch of the Black Mansion, Ellsworth, Maine. (Paul Rocheleau)*

Shaker Rockers

My Mother's wisdom is so rare
In every branch of science
That in her wisdom I can trust
And place a firm reliance.
My Mother is a carpenter
She hews the crooked stick
And she will have it strait and squair
Altho it cuts the quick.
My Mother is a Joiner wise
She builds her spacious dome
And all that trace her sacred ways
Will find a happy home.
—(Quoted from Andrews, *Shaker Furniture*, 1964)

BELOW: *Three Sisters from Sabbathday Lake, Maine, visiting The Shaker Museum at Chatham, New York, 1956. (The Shaker Museum, Chatham, New York)*

This Shaker song associates the image of Mother—or woman—with that of a carpenter and joiner. Women, historically, have been excluded from architectural

training and allied trades. Few women made the pots they decorated. Furniture-making prior to the Shaker movement was an exclusively male sphere.

In the Shaker community, the role of woman was exalted. The religious doctrines of Shakerism were not based on a patriarchal hierarchy. Shakerism emancipated "women from a position of social inferiority, and the investment of the deity with feminine as well as masculine virtues were fundamental principles in the Shaker theology" (Potter and Anthea in *Women's Art Journal*, 1985). Ann Lee, the founder of the Shaker movement in America, was born in England in 1736. She sought salvation through faith and for positive signs for relief from the depressing conditions of her everyday live. Her public criticism of organized religion earned her a jail sentence for disturbing the peace. While serving her sentence she reported a visitation from Jesus. The visitation united her with Jesus as the feminine side of God on earth. In 1774, she emigrated with some followers to America and founded the Shaker movement here.

OPPOSITE: *Blue and white fabric strips have been woven together for the seat of this rocker; the "sewing steps" at the foot of the rocker were used by Shaker seamstresses who rocked while they worked. The Shakers were great fans of rocking chairs, although an extremist Shaker disapprovingly connected their growing popularity among his fellow "Believers" to a desire for more ease. (Hancock Shaker Village, Pittsfield, Massachusetts, Paul Rocheleau)*

ABOVE: *Armed Shaker rocker with baskets and table; when these slat-back rockers first appeared on the market late in the eighteenth century, they sold for about one dollar. Both these chairs have the mushroom handholds seen on later Shaker rockers. (Paul Rocheleau)*

ABOVE: *Armchair from the Shaker community at Mount Lebanon, New York, 1800–30. (Winterthur Museum, Winterthur, Delaware)*

BELOW: *Shaker meeting set up with chairs and benches. (The Shaker Museum, Chatham, New York)*

The Shakers insisted on rules for life that would guarantee salvation: separation of the sexes, communal life, no private property, and celibacy. Every member had a place in the community and a set of duties. The core of the governing body consisted of Elders and Eldresses—usually two of each. They were empowered to make the rules that governed the Believers. This was consistent with the Shaker belief in equality of the sexes. Men and women shared in authority and duty. Men undertook the heavy work of farming and building and women the domestic chores of cleaning and cooking. They shared, however, in the manufacture of goods for sale.

Many of the Shaker communities made rocking chairs. The Shaker chair was an aesthetic metaphor for the religious precepts of the society: simplicity, separation from the world, utilitarianism, and dedication to fine craftsmanship. The three periods associated with furnituremaking in the Shaker sect are: the Primitive Era, which lasted from 1790 to 1820 and was distinguished by furniture that was crude, physically heavy, plain in form, but strong and functional; the Classical Era, from 1820 to 1860, whose expressions of utility, simplicity, and perfection where attributable to spiritual inspiration, moral responsiveness, and dedication to craft—this was the period of greatest creativity and productivity; and the Final Phase, from 1860 to 1935, which was an era of mass production and total reliance on the machine. During this time, we see the gradual decline of furnituremaking due to the decrease of religious dedication and ultimately mem-

bership. Artistically, it is distinguished by a sameness in design. There is evidence in Shaker account books that the sale of chairs played a major role in the economic growth of the society. The range of prices for rocking chairs were recorded in daily journals. Those without arms ranged from $3.00 to $7.50. Those with arms ranged from $3.25 to $8.00. There was no significant increase in the price of rocking chairs for over forty years.

Elder Robert Wagon (1833–83) helped supervise chairmaking at the New Lebanon chair factory. He realized that to meet the ever-growing demands for Shaker chairs and to compete with other chair manufacturers, it would be necessary to update factory machinery, increase productivity, and to advertise. He reorganized production methods and standardized the line of chairs by numbering the chairs according to size. Zero was the smallest child's chair and seven was the largest adult chair. The earliest Shaker furniture catalogue was issued by Elder Robert Wagon in 1874. In it, he warned the public about dealers selling imitation Shaker furniture. To help prevent this, he began affixing a gold trademark decal as a mark of authentication. He also provided instructions on how to remove the decals, if desired, once you had bought an authenticated Shaker chair.

Elder Wagon, for twenty years of his life, ran the Shaker furniture factory. Brother Perkins eventually succeeded him, continuing the traditions established by Elder Wagon. Brother Perkins worked with Eldress Sarah Collins, who took

TOP LEFT: *South Family Shakers, Mount Lebanon, New York. (The Shaker Museum, Chatham, New York)*

ABOVE: *Woven wool or cotton taped seats appeared on Shaker chairs after 1830 and eventually replaced splint seats. (Paul Rocheleau)*

FOLLOWING: *A selection of Shaker chairs—rocking and not. A shawl-top chair on the far wall allowed a cushion or shawl to hang over the back. Chairs were all designed to be light enough to hang on pegs on the wall. (Hancock Shaker Village, Pittsfield Massachusetts, Paul Rocheleau)*

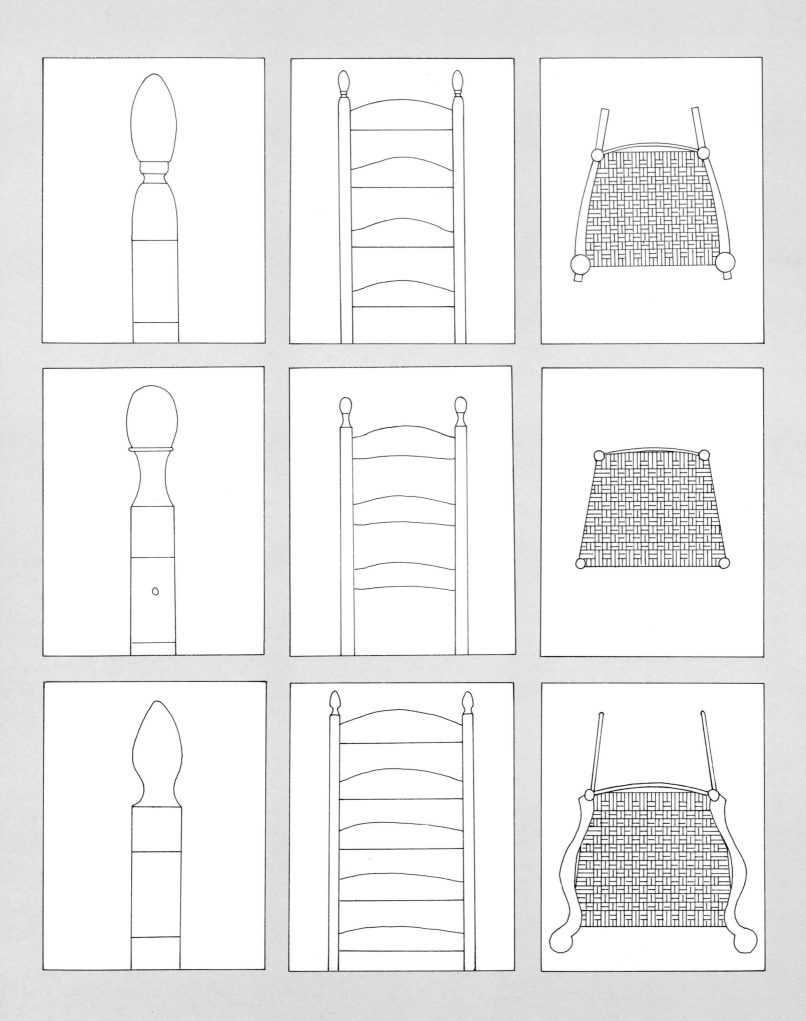

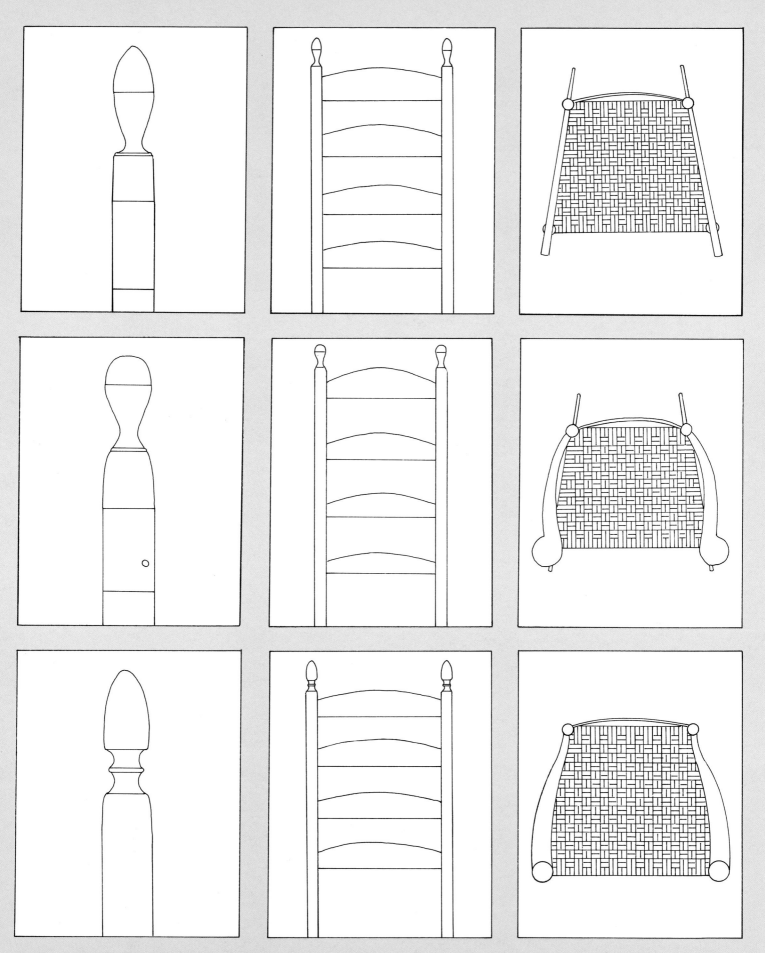

Slight variations in the finials, back slats, and seats of Shaker rockers signify their region of origin; from top to bottom: Mount Lebanon, New York; South Union, Kentucky; North Union, Ohio; Enfield New Hampshire; Sabbathday Lake, Maine; Watervliet, New York. (Nadine Gordon)

ABOVE: *Although these two chairs are*
decidedly not Shaker, the ladder-back
rocker suited the needs of many
Americans, not just the Shakers, and
was frequently seen strapped to the backs
of pioneer wagons heading west. The
undulating turnings on the front legs
and back posts of the chair at right are
known as the "sausage-and-ball" style,
which was seen on ladder-backs made in
New England. (Old Sturbridge Village,
Sturbridge, Massachusetts)

OPPOSITE: *Rockers on the porch of a*
guest house on Sea Island, Georgia.
(Tim Bieber, The Image Bank)

over the running of the chair factory in 1934, assisted by Sister Lillian Barlow. Under the tenure of Elder Wagon and Sister Perkins, sheep were raised and their wool woven into strips used for taping the chair seats. When Eldress Collins and Sister Barlow inherited the supervision of the chair factory, they found it more expedient and less costly to simply purchase the taping materials, ready-made.

Although the Shakers designed rocking chairs for relaxation and occupational needs, more specifically the rocking chair was developed for and used by invalids and the aged. It is ironic that our association today with rocking chairs are related to child-bearing when in fact the Shaker doctrines insisted on celibacy.

The Shaker society was dedicated to expressing an inner devotion and an outward sign of grace. Work was sacred. Perfection in work signified perfection of the spirit. Believers repeated such aphorisms as: "Hands to work and hearts to God" and "Do your work as though it were to last a thousand years, and you were to die tomorrow." These thoughts, attributed to Mother Ann Lee, served almost as mantras. The work and the worker existed in a perfect symbiosis. And as Thomas Merton observed: "The peculiar grace of a Shaker chair is due to the fact that it was made by someone capable of believing that an angel might come and sit on it."

THE BRUMBY JUMBO

Tradition has it that a man had to work two weeks to buy one, but when it was his, he had it for life. When Thomas Brumby produced his first "Jumbo" rocker in 1875, he probably didn't suspect that he had created an American classic. Yet, it is said that Joel Chandler Harris rocked in one as he meditated over his tales of the South (including *Br'er Rabbit*), and that, more recently, former President Jimmy Carter brought five "Jumbos" to the White House during his term in office. The Brumby thrived in its day because it met the demands of an American public that desired a durable and versatile chair that could be used on the front porch as well as in front of the fire. Soon, the Brumby "Jumbo" was a familiar site in the homes of thousands of American families, both inside and outside of Georgia, forcing the Brumby Furniture Company of Marietta to reserve one entire floor of its factory for the chair's construction. (Many a Brumby accompanied settlers on their journey West during a period of rapid national expansion.)

It took twelve craftsmen to make each chair over a period of about five weeks. Although the majority of the work was done by hand, much of the frame was "turned" by machine. A combination of "air-dried" and "kiln-dried" red oak was used in each chair to give it stability and durability. Americans tended to bring the chair outside in the summer and inside during the winter months, and the changes in temperature and humidity tended to weaken the frames of most rockers. This combination of dried red oak, a distinctive feature of the Brumby, compensated for this problem, since air-dried oak tends to contract with changes in weather while kiln-dried oak tends to expand. The two types of wood, then, complemented the fluctuations in the other, with the result that the chair actually "tightened" itself with the change in climate.

The seat and back of the Brumby were made of the finest double-woven cane for strength, and the back posts were curved slightly for comfort, conforming with the back of the seat and accommodating the spine of the sitter. The skates were extra wide and arched slightly in the back, providing an even rocking motion without the threat of the chair tipping over. (Indeed, many rockers were used to rock infants to sleep. The Brumbys attempted to accommodate American mothers by developing and incorporating arched skates into their design.) The armrests were also extra wide (five inches) for "elbow room," and the chair simply decorated with roundels on the back posts and gentle turnings on the frame. The chair stood forty-eight inches high and weighed thirty-two pounds.

The rocker remained popular into the twentieth century and the Brumbys sold as many Jumbos as they could craft. The Jumbo was often included as part of a wife's dowry, and usually retained a prominent position in the new home. In 1942, however, the Brumby factory was forced to discontinue production of the Jumbo since, given the political climate, it was impossible to import any cane from the Far East. (Manpower and domestic raw materials were also reserved for the war effort.) As an indication of how lucrative and popular the Jumbo had become, it should be noted that the Brumby Furniture Company was unable to sustain itself without rocker production and that, two years later, in 1944, it was forced to close its entire factory.

It was not until 1972 that the first new Brumby was completed at the Rocker Shop of Marietta, Georgia. Though Frank and Carole Melson were granted permission in 1967 by the Brumby family to begin production on a new series of the rocker, five long years would pass before Carole Melson felt ready to proceed with her dream. (True to its "mother's-helper" heritage, the Brumby had helped Carole Melson to rock her own sick child to sleep. The Melsons became interested in reviving the chair soon after.) This lapse of time was due, in part, to unforeseeable setbacks, the most devastating of which was the death by heart attack of Frank Melson at age thirty-eight. The Melsons, however,

A ROCKER MADE OF RED OAK BY THE
BRUMBY CHAIR COMPANY IN MARIETTA,
GEORGIA, C. 1875. (THE HIGH MUSEUM OF
ART, ATLANTA, GEORGIA, GIFT OF THE
ROCKER SHOP OF MARIETTA)

had also been determined to follow the Brumby tradition meticulously and, from the beginning, had taken their time learning the history of the chair and the way it was originally made.

The Melsons searched the South for the original Rube Goldberg custom-fit machinery used in 1942 and for craftsmen who had worked in the original Brumby factory. They committed themselves to using the same combination of red oak for the frame, which is dried over a period of two years, as well as the finest Far Eastern cane for the seating. The dimensions of the chair were approximately the same and much of the work was done by hand, including the sanding and bending. In short, the Brumby of 1972 was to duplicate the Brumby of 1942 in every detail. Their success was evidenced by the flood of orders that quickly overwhelmed the small factory for Jumbos.

Nevertheless, there is a significant difference between the two chairs which threatens to halt production for a second time. In 1942, an order of fine red oak cost the company forty-three dollars; the same order costs two thousand today. A Brumby Jumbo, which cost the American buyer twenty-five dollars in 1942, now commands over seven hundred. This dramatic rise in material costs threatens to close the factory even though interest in the chair and the Rocker Shop has been encouraging. Carole Melson has said that she cannot find a supplier with the quantity or, more importantly, quality of wood she needs, and she refuses to substitute for any of the original materials. Consequently, she does not hold much hope that the business will survive.

Although it is this commitment to quality and tradition that characterizes the Brumby chair, this same commitment may ultimately lead to its demise. Happily for all of us, at the time of this writing the Rocker Shop is still advertising the Brumby Jumbo. However, the threat is real, and, quite simply, if we lose the Brumby, we will lose a significant part of our national heritage.

Wicker Rockers

BELOW: *A hand-tinted photograph of Wicker rockers on an Atlanta porch. (Virginia Warren Smith)*

OPPOSITE TOP: *Rustic rockers on a Cape Cod porch. (Brett Froomer, The Image Bank)*

OPPOSITE BOTTOM: *A collection of white rockers. (Al Satterwhite, The Image Bank)*

Wicker first appeared in America aboard the Mayflower in the form of a cradle, which had rocked an infant born during the crossing. While wicker had been commonly used throughout England and the other British colonies—in India, for example, where it was ideal for warm-weather furnishings—it was not until the nineteenth century that it became a popular medium among furnituremakers in America. Then, as a result of new trade relations with China after the Opium Wars, shipments of goods—silks, china, and teas—sailed from the East to the harbors of New England. The goods were safely packed into the ships' holds with rattan to prevent any damage during transit.

A young grocer named Cyrus Wakefield was at Boston Harbor one day when one of these cargo-laden ships arrived. As the merchandise was being unloaded, the dock was strewn with the excess packing material. Wakefield picked up some of it and determined that there had to be some use for the rattan, which would otherwise have been discarded. He carted a sack of it home and began to experiment.

ABOVE: *Carpentry repair workshop at the Tuskgegee Institute, Alabama. (Schomburg Center for Research in Black Culture, The New York Public Library, Astor, Lenox, and Tilden Foundations, C.M. Batty)*

Wakefield soon began buying the huge lots of refuse rattan that came off ships arriving from the Orient and re-sold them to furnituremakers who wove the rattan into caning for chair backs and seats. After amassing a tidy profit through his rattan business, Wakefield moved just north of Boston and opened his own rattan furniture factory, winding rattan around wooden frames. He designed his own chairs, settees, stools, and even floor and table mats in the Victorian style. The malleability of wicker made it particularly appropriate for the decorative flourishes of Victorian tastes and, surprisingly, American wicker furniture soon took on a much more "Victorian" character than wicker furniture coming from England. Like the rocking chair, Europeans viewed wicker as somewhat inferior (it was relatively inexpensive), and relegated it primarily to chair caning rather than actual furnituremaking.

Wicker made from rattan or reed was ideal for warm-weather, outdoor furniture. In rocking form, wicker chairs could rest upon elegant porches and verandahs; they were lightweight and so could be easily transported; and the vagaries of the weather did not seem to damage the material. In the long run, however, rattan did not prove quite so durable and the somewhat cavalier treatment of it over the years has meant that older wicker furniture is now quite rare. (Interestingly, ancient wicker furniture was found in Egyptian tombs, preserved by the peculiar climate of the underground tombs.)

In 1873, Cyrus Wakefield died and his nephew took over the family business, which continued to produce wicker furniture into the 1930s. Even as the taste for Victorian-styled furniture waned in America, wicker furniture manufacturers prospered as the medium proved equally effective for translating the ornate, vine-like motifs popular among Art Nouveau proponents at the turn of the century.

By the 1880s, however, reed replaced the shiny rattan that had been used for so long in wicker furniture. Rattan proved difficult to paint and so was usually left in its natural state, but reed received paint well and thus better suited the current tastes. Once painted, wicker furniture was no longer simply a feature of porches and lawns, but could be brought into the living room. Wicker furniture, painted or not, continues to be an extremely popular furniture style.

LEFT: *A platform rocking chair, made from reed and rattan by the Ordway Chair Company, Framingham, Massachusetts, c. 1895. Ordway's platform rocker was introduced in the late nineteenth century. By placing the rocking mechanism on a stable base, the chairs did not move across the floor when in motion. This mechanical innovation was combined with the renewed enthusiasm for reed furniture at the end of the century. (Virginia Carroll Crawford Collection, Permanent Collection of the High Museum of Art, Atlanta, Georgia)*

RIGHT: *White-painted Victorian wicker has been seen on porches since the 1880s. (Bruce Wodder, The Image Bank)*

OPPOSITE: *Wicker rocker made by Cyrus Wakefield in 1880. (Gift of Loran Cash in memory of Michael L. Botts, Permanent Collection of the High Museum of Art, Atlanta, Georgia, Lucinda Bunnen)*

ABOVE AND OPPOSITE: *White wicker in a Southern spring and a New England fall.*
(Bruce Wolf and Chris Hackett, The Image Bank)

FOLLOWING: *A country living room with wicker and Adirondack-style chairs. (Chris Mead)*

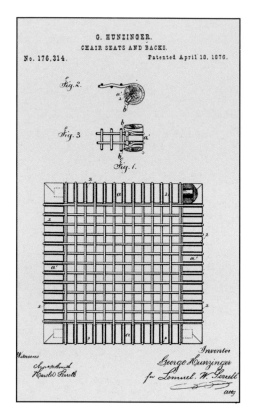

G. HUNZINGER.
CHAIR SEATS AND BACKS.
No. 176,314. *Patented April 18. 1876.*

ABOVE: *Drawing of George Hunzinger's patented wire mesh design for chair seats and backs. (United States Patent Office)*

As beloved as the rocking chair came to be in American society, it was also the subject of criticism. The skates were often clumsy and took up too much room, preventing the chair from being shoved close to the wall and out of the way. These problems were solved by the platform rocker, which was also primarily responsible for elevating the rocking chair to the level of fine or "fancy" furniture.

The platform rocker flourished in the 1870s and met the quickly changing demands of an industrialized America. The rocking chair had come to be perceived as a passive piece of furniture, its design emphasizing comfort over elegance, suitable for the open-air porch but not for the parlor. Chair manufacturers experimented with all types of new designs in an attempt to make the rocker more acceptable and earn a place in this blossoming market. These included ornamental fabric covers for seat and back, fine wood frames (such as mahogany), and classical styles. In a short period, for example, American design trends included Gothic (1830–65), Rococo (1844–63), and Renaissance (1855–75) revivals.

The single most important innovation, however, which successfully bridged the gap between "friendly" and "fancy" furniture was the technical development of a stationary base, which allowed the chair to rock noiselessly, without skating along the floor. The base replaced the long, cumbersome traditional rockers and added stability to the overall design.

The enormous popularity and demand for this new chair compelled manufacturers to patent their designs in an effort to discourage would-be imitators. Manufacturers began to stamp their furniture with their names and addresses, as well

RIGHT: *Hunzinger's wire mesh invention may have inspired Harry Bertoia's* Diamond Chair, *1952, manufactured by Knoll International. (Knoll Studio, a division of the Knoll Group)*

OPPOSITE: *Patent drawing for Hunzinger's Spring Rocking Chair, September 26, 1882. (United States Patent Office)*

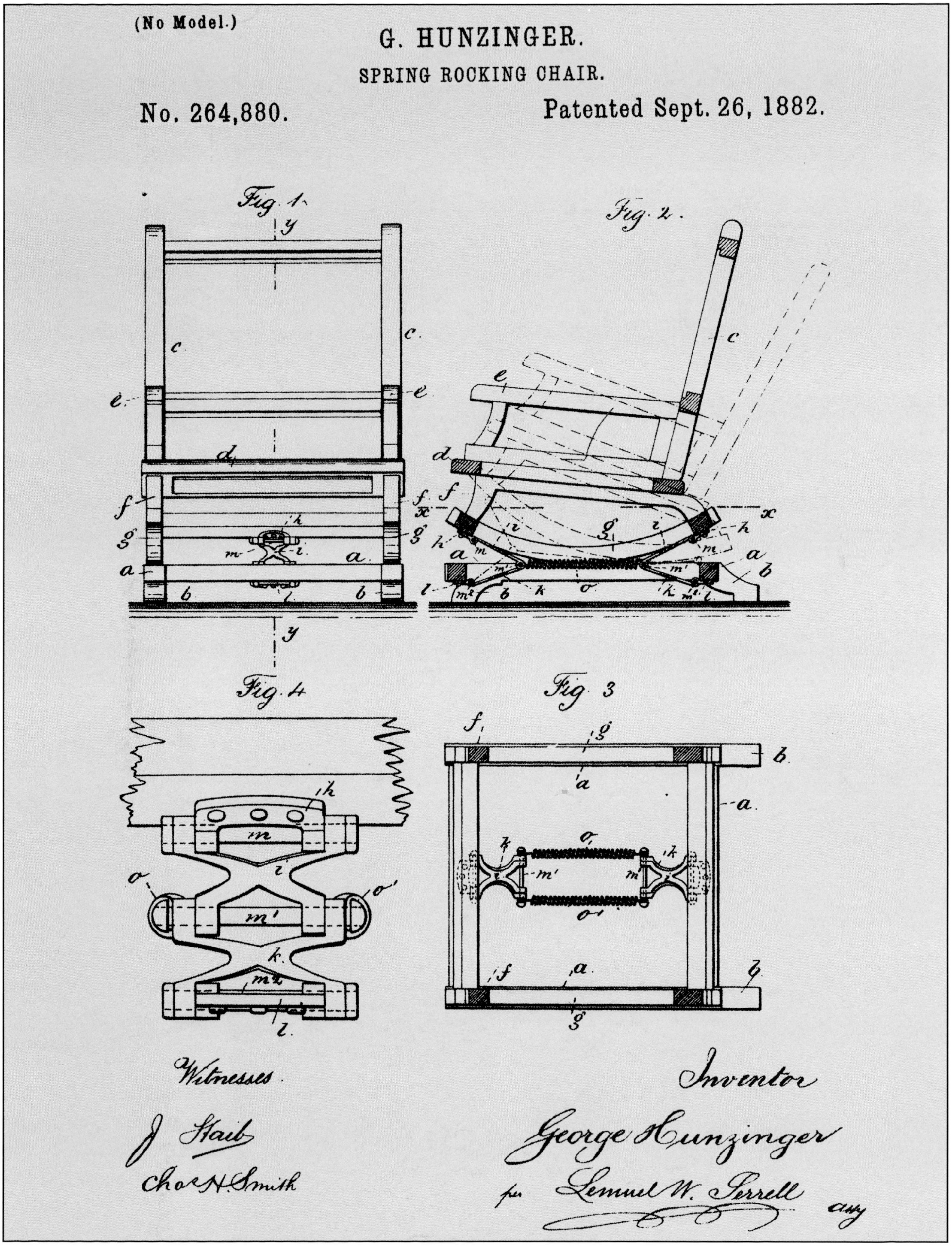
(No Model.)
G. HUNZINGER.
SPRING ROCKING CHAIR.
No. 264,880.
Patented Sept. 26, 1882.
Fig. 1.
Fig. 2.
Fig. 4
Fig. 3
Witnesses.
J Staib
Chas H. Smith
Inventor
George Hunzinger
per Lemuel W. Serrell
atty

GEORGE HUNZINGER

A German immigrant who settled in Brooklyn in the 1850s, Hunzinger was born in Tuttlingen, near the Swiss border in 1835, and came from a family of cabinetmakers, who had worked in the area since 1612. (The Hunzingers continue to manufacture furniture in this small town to this day.) Following his apprenticeship, he left home and spent much of his time as a journeyman in Geneva. He soon followed a wave of German immigrants to America and found work in the furniture trade, which at the time was strongly Germanic. In Brooklyn, he met Marie Susanne Grieb, also from Tuttlingen, and the two married on Christmas Day, 1859. Hunzinger received his United States citizenship in 1865.

In all, Hunzinger received twenty furniture patents over the course of thirty years. His first, for a reclining chair with footboard that could serve as a table, was obtained in 1861. (The entire unit could be folded for transport.) In 1866, he obtained another patent for a folding chair (one of his most successful) and in 1869 for a folding chair with a diagonal side brace for strength. Hunzinger soon realized that he

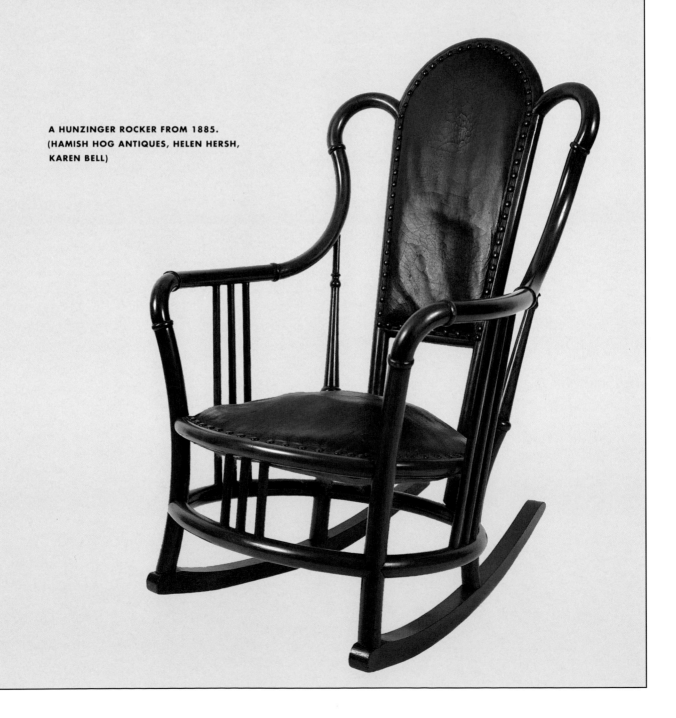

A HUNZINGER ROCKER FROM 1885.
(HAMISH HOG ANTIQUES, HELEN HERSH,
KAREN BELL)

A PLATFORM ROCKER DESIGNED BY
HUNZINGER; THE TRADITIONAL ROCKER
WAS REPLACED IN THE 1870S BY THE
PLATFORM ROCKER. (PRIVATE COLLECTION,
NEW YORK, KAREN BELL)

was able to patent parts of his chairs and several of his patents are solely for strong structural systems and mechanisms. One notable accomplishment was a patent for a wire mesh seat and back, in place of caning. Hunzinger originally incorporated this design, with machine-like roundels and turnings, in an armchair in 1876, a rocker version. The mesh was attached to the chair frame by a series of grooves and pins connected to a wire band. This innovative design appears to be the forerunner of such later wire furniture as the wire mesh chair of Harry Bertoia, made earlier this century. Hunzinger's patented platform—or spring—rocker, however, became his most popular invention. He continued to be concerned with the durability of his furniture and to combine comfort, elegance, and function into his designs.

In 1873, based on his successes, he moved from 402 Bleecker Street to Seventh Avenue, between 18th and 19th Streets. In 1877, Hunzinger's factory was destroyed by fire. His insurance was not adequate and forced him to temporarily house his factory in three locations over the next two years. His recovery from fire and the firm's continued prosperity were due primarily to his experiments with the spring rocker. In 1879, he was able to move into a new building on West 16th Street, which still stands today.

Sotheby's recently sold a Hunzinger for close to forty-five thousand dollars.

as patent numbers and dates, which added caché to the chair while assuring the client of its uniqueness. The prestige or status associated with owning such an authentically labeled article was not lost on the American buyer, and patent furnituremakers thrived financially into the next century.

One of the most successful patent furniture manufacturers was George Hunzinger. The Hunzinger platform rocker was not patented until 1882 although he had experimented with its design in the 1870s. Forerunners included Gardner & Company of New York, which patented iron supports for a platform rocker as early as 1872, and Heywood Brothers & Company of Massachusetts, which patented a platform rocker in 1873.

Although not the first designer, Hunzinger is widely regarded as the father of the platform rocker for his innovative spring and hinge movement, absent in the Gardner or Heywood chairs, which, as he explained in his patent appli-

CHARLES LOCK EASTLAKE

A PLATFORM ROCKER OF EBONIZED WOOD, PHILADELPHIA, C. 1870-80; THE DESIGN WAS RECOMMENDED BY EASTLAKE HIMSELF; THE WOOD HAS BEEN ELABORATELY CARVED IN RENAISSANCE-REVIVAL STYLE. (SMITHSONIAN INSTITUTION, WASHINGTON, D.C.)

A furniture style popular in America late in the nineteenth century came to be known as "Eastlake Victorian," after its proponent, the English furniture designer Charles Lock Eastlake. Born in Devonshire in 1836, Eastlake traveled extensively as a young man, studying the Medieval architecture of Europe; he went on to become the secretary of the Royal Institute of British Architects and later, keeper of the National Gallery in London.

Like his fellow design reformers, William Morris and John Ruskin, Eastlake greatly admired the craftsmanship and principles of Gothic architecture. During a time when taste for furniture in Victorian England was verging on the over-stuffed and gaudy, Eastlake called for a paring down of decoration and lines and a return to the solid, finely crafted furniture of the Middle Ages.

In 1868, he published his highly influential *Hints on Household Taste in Furniture, Upholstery, and Other Details;* the furniture designs included were largely rectilinear, often enhanced with spindling and relief carving. When this book was published in America in the 1870s, it was greeted with still more enthusiasm than in England. The "art furniture" that he praised became a sign of taste and the term "Eastlake" began to be used freely late in the century. It was often applied to furniture that certainly did not bear the stamp of approval of the man himself— this platform rocker, however, was, indeed, "recommended" by Eastlake. Although greatly diluted by 1900, the style of furniture that Eastlake had first inspired was one of the most popular design trends in the last decades of the nineteenth century.

cation,"insures a stable connection of the parts, and at the same time a positive and easy spring movement." This allowed the sitter to rock back and forth comfortably and noiselessly. Also notable are the corkscrew braces connecting the arms and back to the seat, and the reiterated circles which ornament the chair and support the arm rests and back. The spring rocker, as it was also known, proved to be very popular and Hunzinger's most lucrative invention.

ABOVE: *Hunzinger rocker. (Private collection, New York, Andrew Wainwright)*

OPPOSITE: *Platform rocker on the porch of Robert Frost's Farm, Franconia, New Hampshire. (Paul Rocheleau)*

Inspired by the Arts and Crafts movement in England at the end of the nineteenth century, American artisans sought a return to crafts worked by hand. Many of their designs were based on the architecture of Native Americans and the Spanish missions in the southwest part of the country, which incorporated native materials and pure, clean lines. Gustav Stickley was one of the leaders of the movement in America. In 1910, he published the first issue of *The Craftsman*, a magazine devoted to the explication of the philosophy of the Arts and Crafts movement and to the visual representation of its (at the time) revolutionary furniture and architectural designs. (The furniture made by the proponents of this movement were known as "Craftsman," after Stickley's journal.)

Not surprisingly, Stickley dedicated this first issue to the works and ideas of William Morris, the true father of that movement. Morris' influence was extensive, and it inspired a number of independent *Craftsman* journals, exhibitions, and cooperative production guilds and communities in England as well as America. The most important effects of his influence, which did much to inspire American designers, were the publication of the magazine *Studio* in 1893 and the formation, among others, of the Arts Worker's Guild in 1884 and the Guild of Handicraft in 1888. *Studio,* which, much like Stickley's publication, was devoted to the pictorial representation of Arts and Crafts products, soon had its American counterparts in *The House Beautiful* (1896) and *International Studio* (1897). The Guilds held annual exhibitions of Arts and Crafts products from 1888 to1890 in a format designed to allow the masses to enjoy their designs as much as the upper classes. The Arts and Crafts Exhibition Society was created in 1888, from which the entire movement took its name.

Like Arts and Crafts furniture, Craftsman products are also based on simplicity and a concern for the general public, and indeed, at the onset, Stickley and his followers were producing high quality furniture at affordable prices. Their designs reflected a pure, sometimes austere, hardworking quality of American life. They rejected ornament, dedicating their efforts, instead, to the utility of design. In the chairs and rockers, this was evident in large armrests, slat-backs, and "stick" designs. The attachments of the legs and seats were exposed; the seats, often covered with leather, were fastened with heavy tacks, which were also exposed. The wood was finished with dark stains, which accentuated the grain, drawing attention to the material itself. Though perhaps intimidating, Mission-style furnishings remain beautiful pieces of Americana.

OPPOSITE: *Although the curving skate would seem to defy the rectilinear tastes of Mission-style furnituremakers, the rocking chair was actually a popular design among them. (Henry Ford Museum & Greenfield Village, Dearborn, Michigan)*

GUSTAV STICKLEY

ARTS AND CRAFTS ROCKER MADE BY
L. AND J.G. STICKLEY OF OAK AND LEATHER
IN 1905. (GALLERY 520, NEW YORK)

Gustav Stickley's rise to the top of the American Arts and Crafts movement (he later coined the term "Craftsman") was a rather rocky one. He was born on March 9, 1858, in Osceola, Wisconsin, to German immigrant parents who changed the family name from Stoeckel to Stickley. By the age of twelve, Gustav had already mastered the work of a stonemason's apprentice (under his father), an experience so hard on him that in his later architectural designs he rarely ever used cut stone. When Stickley's father abandoned them in the 1870s, the family moved to Pennsylvania where Gustav took responsibility for their welfare. It was here, at the Brandt Chair Company of Brandt, Pennsylvania, that Gustav had his first experience working with wood and making furniture.

In 1884, Stickley and his two younger brothers moved to Binghamton, New York, to establish a wholesale/retail furniture business where they sold "fancy" chairs, Brandt chairs, and Shaker furniture. Gustav began to design what would evolve into his Craftsman style. The firm did not have enough money to buy machinery, so Stickley rented the lathe of a local broom-handle maker and put together some chairs in the "Shaker" style. Although the work was hard and time consuming, Stickley saw this as an opportunity to break away from machine-made forms common in the period.

At about this time, Gustav Stickley met and married Eda Ann Simmons, a story so romantic that it is hard not to include it here. After the death of Eda's mother, she was placed in a convent by her father John Simmons. Gustav and Eda somehow met while she was at the convent and fell in love. With the help of a milkman that serviced the convent, Gustav and Eda began a clandestine correspondence, and a few months later in September, again with the help of the milkman, Eda escaped and the two were married.

Stickley left his brothers to form a partnership with Elgin A. Simonds; the chair shown here was made by the brothers' firm. The original Stickley-Simonds company lasted only two years, and from 1891 to 1894 Stickley held a variety of jobs outside of the furniture industry. In 1891, for example, he was made vice-president of the Binghamton Street Railroad. From 1892 to 1894 he was director of manufacturing operations at the New York State Prison at Auburn. Although Stickley made use of prison labor to create a number of simple wooden chairs, he is remembered at the prison for one in particular: the electric chair, which he designed and which is still in place at the prison today. While still at Auburn, he and Simonds bought property in Syracuse and by 1896 the Stickley-Simonds Company was firmly established. The age of Craftsman furniture was at hand.

*Mahogany rocker in the Gamble
House, Pasadena, California,
designed by S. and Henry M. Greene
and manufactured by the Peter Hall
Manufacturing Company of Pasadena.
(Tim Street-Porter)*

Adirondack Rockers

Although the Adirondacks were settled as early as the 1820s, the great rustic mountain houses and lodges did not flourish in the area until the end of the Civil War. (It is difficult to imagine, yet this great American crisis seemed to have little or no effect on the plans of prominent families who sought the calming environment of the Adirondack Mountains.) At this time, city life became increasingly hectic and stressful as Americans endeavored to accumulate great wealth through business. Middle- and upper-class families began to seek refuge in natural surroundings and wilderness retreats, and built vacation homes that mixed the formalities of Victorian decorum with the rural simplicity of country life. As the summer retreat became a national institution, homes were built that reflected this spiritual transformation.

The Adirondack "camp," which before the 1870s was used to describe a series of shanties and log cabins grouped in one area, now signified the great estates of the Vanderbilts and Morgans, designed by such architects as W.W. Durant, William Coulter, and Robert Robertson. As William Dix explained in 1903 in *The Independent,* the Adirondack camp was "a permanent home where the fortunate owners assemble for several weeks each year and live in perfect comfort and even luxury, though in the heart of the woods. . . ." Although the "fortunate owners" would have described their dwellings as rustic, it is important to distinguish, especially with regard to furniture, between true rustic (including "ramshackle rustic") and what George Leland Hunter, a Victorian writer on the decorative arts, termed "polite rusticity."

Original or true rustic furniture was born of necessity and was hand-crafted by woodsmen and hunters for their lean-tos and cabins. Since the emphasis of such furniture was function, the pieces are often crudely built from materials (primarily yellow and white birch, some hickory, cedar, and ash, as well as pine boards) gathered at hand and tied or nailed together. Although often uncomfortable and certainly inelegant, these "ramshackle rustic" pieces are probably the best examples of "original" Adirondack furniture and are valuable for their original, "one-of-a-kind" quality—though perhaps not a decorator's first choice.

"Polite" or fancy rustic describes the mingling of rustic sensibilities with the formalism of Victorian designs and is a direct result of the transition of the "camp" from shanty to lodge house. Furniture of this type approached the rough, asymmetrical, ambiguous lines of rustic but retained a sophistication that placed it well above ramshackle. Such "finished" raw pieces seem founded upon contradic-

ABOVE AND OPPOSITE: *Four styles of rustic Adirondack rockers: this is a design similar to the one used by the Old Hickory Chair Company of Martinsville, Indiana, around the turn of the century; not all "Adirondack" chairs were made in the Adirondack mountains. (Nadine Gordon)*

LEFT: *A variation of the Westport chair, this design, patented by Henry C. Bunnell in 1922, converts into a rocker.*

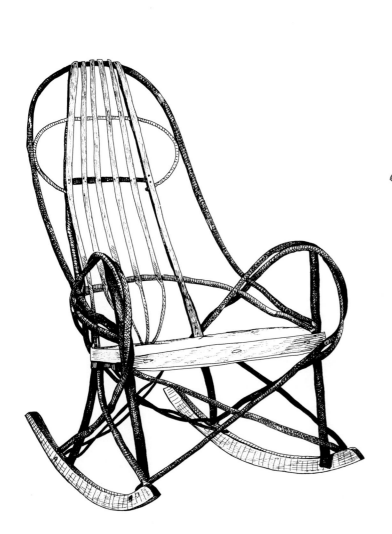

LEFT AND ABOVE: *The delicate lines of these bentwood rockers make them seem unlikely accompaniments to rustic living, but their hickory limbs are actually exceedingly strong; above is a style of rocker made by the Amish in America.*

RIGHT: *Adirondack twig rocker from 1915; these bentwood rockers were generally made of hickory and willow for outdoor use; the market for rustic rockers increased dramatically at the turn of the century as affluent city dwellers escaped to their country fishing and hunting lodges for weekends. (Private collection, New York, Karen Bell)*

OPPOSITE: *West Virginia rocker made by H. Wilson in 1895. (Gift of James Allen, The High Museum of Art, Atlanta, Georgia, Lucinda Bunnen)*

BELOW: *A country living room fitted with two birch rockers with woven wood splint backs and seats. (Chris Mead)*

tion, yet it is interesting to note that this type of furniture began to be accepted within the household and may have contributed to a loosening of formality in Victorian taste in the country as well as the city.

Adirondack furniture (also called Adirondack tree furniture) is especially remarkable for its style and techniques. Early craftsmen generally used entire trees and incorporated all parts in their pieces. Of special interest are Adirondack "stick" chairs, rustic cedar chairs and tables, furniture made from peeled branches of trees (called Peeled-pole), tree burl tables, and applied bark interiors. As demand grew, however, these local craftsmen were displaced by an enormous surge of chairs shipped from outside the Adirondack region.

Although hickory is abundant in the region, "true" Adirondack rocking chairs were made of yellow birch owing to its strength, reddish color, and leather-like texture. Ash and sapling elm were also used for seat and back. Hickory also provided the rocker with a sturdy, durable frame, and the polish of the factory-made chairs was attractive to the Adirondack camper. The seats were often woven from inner bark. Soon, a wave of hickory rockers flooded the area. Much of what is called Adirondack, then, probably originated outside of the area, perhaps Indiana, where the Old Hickory Chair Company and the Indiana Furniture Company were well established. In attempting to satisfy the demand for authentic Adirondack "style" furniture, it appears in retrospect that many of these outside factories actually defined the style.

Also found in the region are bentwood rockers, which are named for the elaborate frames made of saplings and branches which are bent into arcs and loops. The two principal types of bentwood rockers are the "fancy" (named for the reiterated arc and loop patterns that added ornament as well as strength to the frame) and the Amish type which appeared later, probably as early at the 1880s. However, examples of bentwood chairs have been found in the Adirondacks that are apparently the work of Native Americans from Florida. Called "Florida cypress chairs," they also incorporate bentwood for seat and back.

Fancy bentwood chairs are primarily of hickory and willow construction and were generally restricted to outside use. Apparently, the rough design of the frame did not mesh well with Victorian interiors. Many of these chairs were made from "second growth hickory," new growth from the stump of a cut hickory, which tended to slow their manufacture. Although the hickory wood endured well, these chairs have become fragile with age because of the incorporated willow withes. At the time, the Old Hickory Chair Company, which produced many hickory bentwood rockers, warned in their catalogue "not [to] compare these pieces with willow, cane, rush or other cheap goods. . . ." Furniture companies began to stamp their chairs with the name of the firm to insure authenticity.

The Amish bentwood rocker boasts an all-hickory frame and is a simplified

OPPOSITE: *Coal miner's house in Scott's Run, West Virginia, 1935. (Walker Evans, Library of Congress)*

RIGHT: *A yellow birch rocker beside a basket of forsythia. (Chris Mead)*

BELOW: *This curvilinear rocker style was known as "fancy" bentwood; its twigs were probably intertwined while green and then nailed into place. (Chris Mead)*

OPPOSITE: *A very literal "twig" rocker. (Chris Mead)*

BELOW AND RIGHT: *An Adirondack- style chair with lovely lines and woven arms curving out of the back and an eccentric child's rocker with knobby branches. (Chris Mead)*

version of the fancy chair. The all-hickory construction requires less material for back and seat than the fancy, and the Amish substitutes oak or ash for willow. The Amish rocker emphasizes function and form with a sensitivity to line. Unlike the fancy bentwood, the back of the Amish rocker gently arches backward, providing the sitter with more comfort. The best examples of these rockers have remained sturdy over the years.

Another popular chair in the Adirondack region was shipped from nearby Mottville, New York, near Syracuse. F. A. Sinclair began to manufacture practical chairs, which he labelled "Common Sense" chairs, suitable for homes, assembly halls, and schools. The Mottville Chair, as it has become known, was "lathe-turned" (like Shaker chairs) and was distinguished by its durability, lightness, and simplicity of design. Sinclair's first company, Union Chair Works, opened in 1865 and manufactured rockers distinguished by incised black bands on the frame and legs. The rockers also incorporated cane backs and seats.

Two other types of chairs are noteworthy because of their popularity in the region. Mission furniture, which developed in the western part of the country came to be very popular in eastern mountain homes as a way of bringing the "roughness" of the country indoors. The furniture was of simple plank design and made primarily of sturdy oak stained dark brown. Frequently, the backs and seats were of leather and the joints accentuated with heavily wrought hardware. In *Craftsman Homes*, a collection of essays either written by Stickley or under his direction, he described the fundamental principles underlying Mission furniture as "simplicity, durability, and fitness for the life that is to be lived in the house and harmony with its natural surroundings." While it was not renowned for its comfort, its emulation of rural simplicity appealed to city dwellers who wanted a true country experience on their weekends in the mountains.

The second type of chair is of certifiable Adirondack origin and derives its name from the town of Westport, New York. Unlike the Adirondack chair, with which it is often confused, the Westport chair is constructed of boards (rather than slats) and is heavier and larger in proportion. It was the invention of Thomas Lee who, according to locals including Lee's niece, sought to make for himself a comfortable outdoor chair. Yet, Lee did not patent his invention which was instead filed under the name of Henry Bunnell, also of Westport, in 1904.

FOLLOWING: *Adirondack chair overlooking the sea. (Si Chi Ko, The Image Bank)*

Molded polyester provided Eames with a light-weight shell which he then shaped to suit the human body. The shell was attached with rubber shock mounts to wire; the wire braced the legs and the wooden rockers. Eames designed two rocking chairs: RAR and RKR— both manufactured by Herman Miller, Inc. These rockers represented an important step in developing durable and inexpensive furniture in this country. The RKR wire chair, with wire rod structure and birch rockers, was manufactured from 1952 through 1955. (Gift of Barry Friedman and Patricia Pastor, The High Museum of Art, Atlanta, Georgia)

Over two hundred years after the first rockers were made in this country, the chair continues to be a form that inspires furnituremakers, designers, sculptors, painters, and architects today. Their various interpretations are both traditional and completely outlandish—in some cases the original rocker form is positively unrecognizable.

While the rocking chairs of Sam Maloof, Jeremy Singley, and Robert Whitley are based on a style that our colonial cabinetmakers would certainly have recognized, they explore the form with a more sensuous attention to line and media. Such rockers as Trent Hickmon's *Let's Rock* or Helen Brandt's *Two-Seated Rocking Drum*, however, pay only the slightest tribute to designs of past centuries. And designers like David Best and Steven Tucker, whose rockers are completely non-functional, seem to purge themselves completely of old traditions. The image of the rocker has also been incorporated into the work of many American painters and sculptors to whom it signifies a return to tranquil times, thoughts of youth or motherhood, or just a vestige of remaining traditional American values.

Many of these rockers serve functions beyond the obvious sedentary ones. The artsit Tom Miller plays on stereotypes of American blacks in his rockers with watermelon-shaped skates and in *Poet,* Ron Wyffels explores his thoughts of gravity and the roundness of the world. These contemporary rockers are made of wood—both found, such as the wood destined for the fireplace in Beverly Buchanan's chair to the exquisite, carefully sought myrtle burl of George Nakashima's rocker—steel, bronze, and leather—or simply paint on canvas.

The rocker is still, indeed, a most democratic and well-loved piece of furniture; contemporary rocking chair designers continue to produce for presidents, as well as the rest of us.

LEFT AND BELOW:
The RAR molded plastic armchair rocker was manufactured from 1950 through 1968; from 1968 through 1984 it was only available to employees upon the birth or adoption of a child. (Charles Eames Archives, Herman Miller, Inc. and Gift of Kent Hofmann, The High Museum of Art, Atlanta, Georgia)

Functional Rockers

While they may not always appear to be—all the following rocking chairs, designed by a range of furnituremakers, jewelry designers, and architects are functional; they can both be used and admired.

SAM MALOOF
DOUBLE FIDDLE-BACKED ROCKER AND WALNUT ROCKER

Maloof was one of the leading figures in the Crafts Revival movement of the 1950s;
his beautifully carved furniture explores traditional forms. "Working a rough piece of
wood into a complete object," writes the artist, "is the welding together of man and
material."
(Gene Sasse)

*The continuous lines of this rocker,
which echo the sensuous human form,
make its name most appropriate.*

WHITLEY STRAIGHT BACK AND BENT BACK ROCKERS

Both of these chairs are made of figured walnut. They combine structural beauty with strength and function. Their luxuriously contoured surfaces are held together by interlocking joints.

**ANDREW KALINIAK
ROCKING CHAIR**

*Kaliniak does not reinterpret the
traditional rocking chair, but approaches
the form as an entirely new one. Using a
method called compound laminate
bending, he was able to reproduce an
uninterrupted continuity in the lines of
the white ash. (Sybaris Gallery, Royal
Oak, Michigan)*

DAVID N. EBNER

*This rocker is made of red oak with cane
back and seat. The design was inspired
by the sternum bone of birds of flight.
The structural qualities of this bone are
the basis of this chair design. Ebner
interprets traditional furniture forms by
removing embellishments and using
classical proportions. (Bill Apton)*

GREG HARKINS

Harkins preserves the art of handmade chairs in his one man shop in Vaughan, Mississippi. He is known for his Plantation, Double, Nanny (a cradle attached to the side of an adult-sized chair), and Children's rockers, which he makes in oak or walnut. Harkins' rocking chair proves definitively that the rocking chair is the most democratized piece of furniture in rocking existence. Harkins has made rocking chairs for presidents Ronald Reagan, George Bush, and vice president Dan Quayle, as well as astronaut John Glenn, senators, representatives, Bob Hope, George Burns, and even Pope John Paul II—but mostly for "common folk."

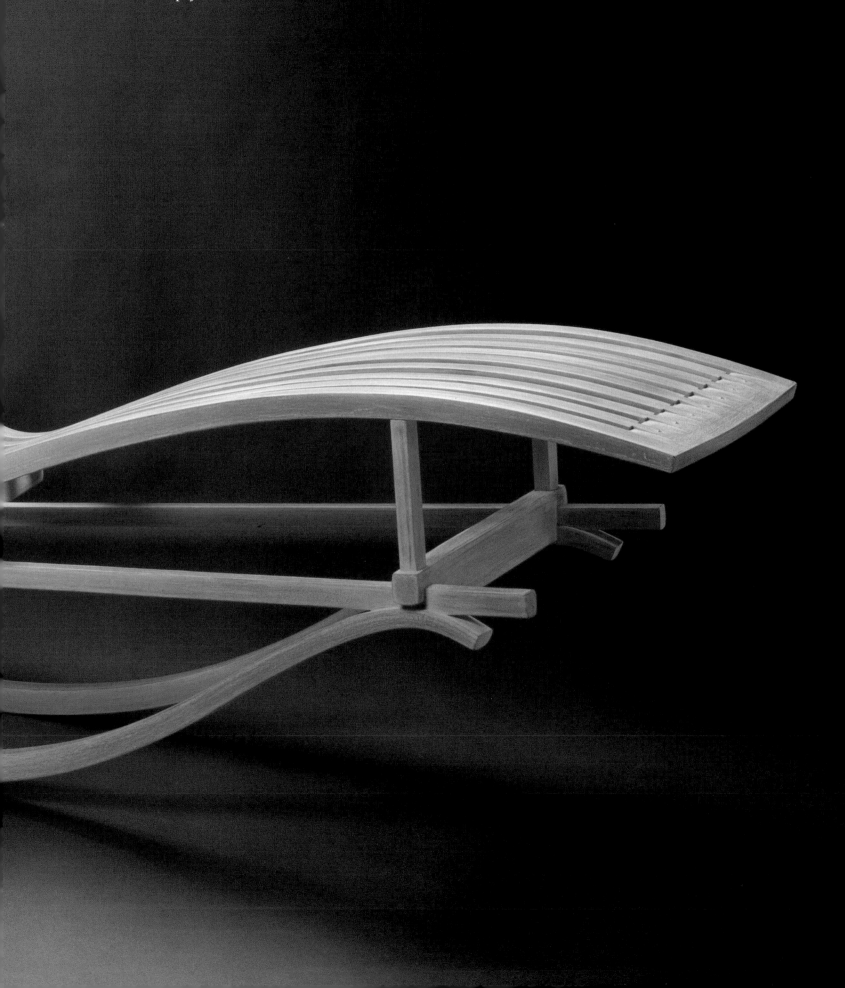

MICHAEL HURWITZ
CHAISE LOUNGE ON ROCKER

Hurwitz's chaise lounge was inspired by steam-bent furniture construction of the 1890s. Although unpretentious in conception, rocking chairs are by no means simple to make. In his delicately rounded chair, Hurwitz deals successfully with the struggle to find visual, as well as physical balance.

JOHN BICKEL

Bickel's black walnut rocking chair deals abstractly with the divergence of the tree branch and the convergence of the tree's root system. The chair is composed of ninety separate pieces and the quality of craftsmanship, as well the respect given to the wood, makes the chair comfortable, sound, enduring, and visually pleasing.

JEREMY SINGLEY HIGH-BACK ROCKING CHAIR

Singley's innovation is the coopered seat—which is extra-deep and wraps around the sitter's legs; it is entirely hand-crafted, and the materials employed are cherry or walnut. The spindles are urn-shaped to fit the lower back. The three outer spindles on either side of the chair are the supporting structures and are made of hickory—a particularly strong wood. The middle spindles are elm—a softer wood that freely flexes in sliding joints.

GEORGE NAKASHIMA
THE LOUNGE CHAIR WITH
FREE-FORM ARM

This design from 1962 is reminiscent of the nineteenth-century Windsor writing armchair, but its lower legs and cleaner lines give it a more contemporary look. The assembly and the individual parts are a collaborative effort between George Nakashima, Jonathan Yarnall (a craftsman in the Nakashima shop), and Mira Nakashima Yarnall.

The arm of the chair is made from rare myrtle burl from Oregon. The shimmering, rippling grain pattern and natural free edge contrast with the seemingly stark lines of the rest of the chair. The back is steam-bent and sanded by hand; the spindles are shaved and trimmed using a Japanese handsaw and chisel. The seat is made of eastern black walnut.

CARLOS RIART, RIART ROCKER

Carlos Riart designed the Riart chair which was manufactured by Knoll International in 1982. It is a well-balanced rocking chair with generous upholstery. The chair was constructed from two types of wood. The decoration of the Brazilian amaranth and ebony frame was mother-of-pearl, while the American holly frame was decorated with ebony inlays. (Knoll Studio, a division of the Knoll Group)

DONALD E. GREEN
This chair integrates the rocker into the structure of the chair so seemlessly that it does not appear to be a four-legged chair on rockers. The traditionally joined chair is made of mahogany and leather with milk paint.

GEORGE GORDON

The gracefully shaped wooden members of Gordon's elegant rocker combine to form a structure that expresses the dynamic simplicity of the rocking motion. The wave-like patterns in the curly maple echo the movement of the chair.

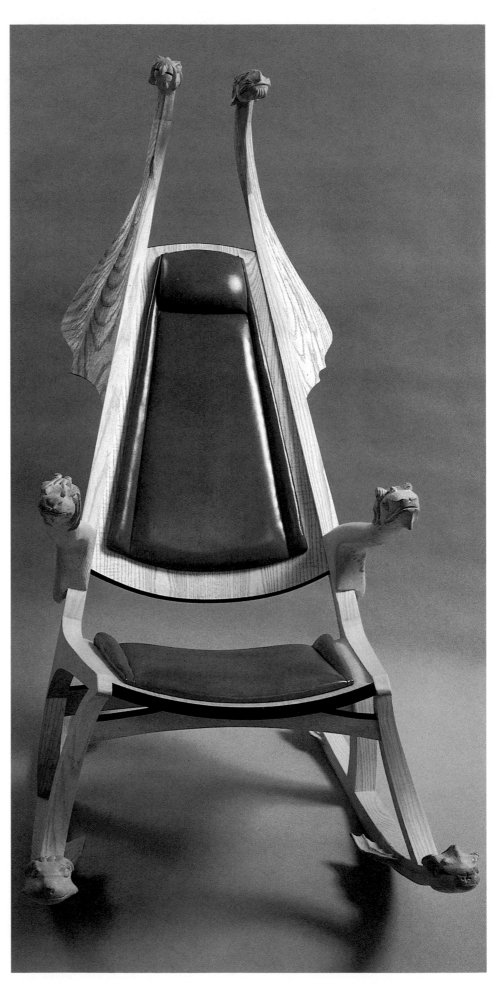

DAVID C. PAGE
SERPENTINE ROCKER

David Page's fantasy rocking chair is both imposing and threatening. Only a brazen viewer dares to sit within the mouth of the serpent. This striking chair is made of ash, ebony, and leather, with a figured ash veneer.

MARCO PASANELLA, ROCKING CHAIR

Marco Pasanella's chair updates the classic rocking chair with a twist—or a tilt—sideways. It is available in solid oak with natural lacquer or milk paint finishes.

BRIAN VANDELLYN PARK, FLOGISTON CHAIR

Brian Vandellyn Park, an engineer, will custom fit his "Flogiston Chair" to your body. Park feels that your mind focuses more sharply when your body is balanced. The chair takes a load off your mind, while reducing the stress on your back. The "Flogiston Chair" featured (the name derives from the word "phlogiston," the first modern scientific theory of energy and combustion) is from the collection of Peter Granger who is six feet two inches and weighs just under two hundred pounds. It was constructed of aluminum, foam, and leather with brass and stainless steel detailing. (Randal Alhadef)

GREGG FLEISHMAN LUMBAREST

Fleishman, an architecturally trained chairmaker, is intrigued by structural systems. The Lumbarest rocker is an exceptionally flexible chair, router-cut from tough Finland birch in his own pattern of continuous "planer springs." The design of the chair is pragmatic and comfortable. (Gallery of Functional Art, Santa Monica, California, Philip Thompson)

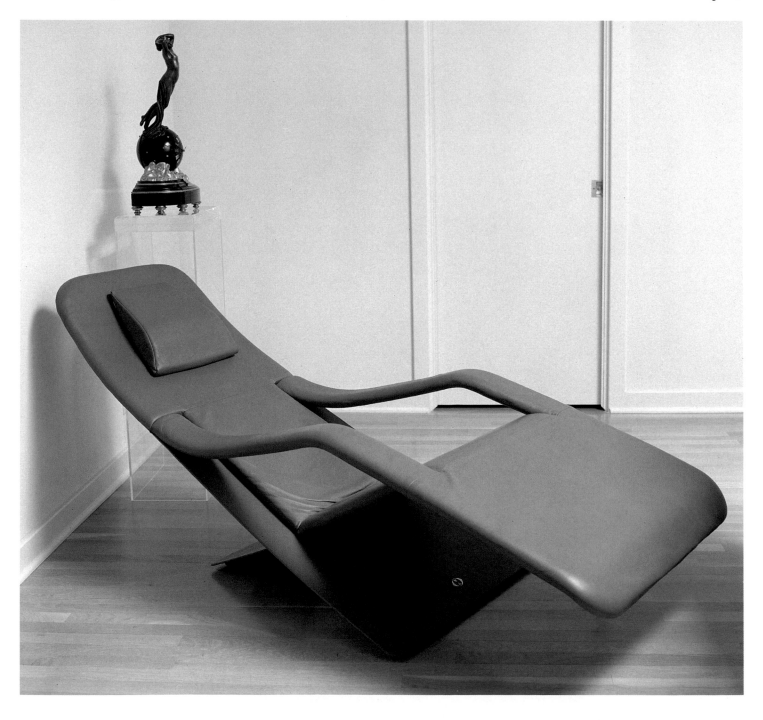

NORMAN PETERSEN
HARD ROCKER

Petersen's Hard Rocker, constructed from steel tubing, with feather-filled canvas or leather upholstery, is an elegant piece of furniture that looks European by way of California. (Sybaris Gallery, Royal Oak, Michigan)

GAIL SMITH
GRAPHITE TO TASTE

Fredell's steel rocker is as much a piece of sculpture as it is a comfortable piece of furniture. (Valerie Massey)

DAVID TISDALE

David Tisdale designs jewelry and table-top accessories, primarily in aluminum. This rocking chair is a continuation of his explorations of color and form. Seams and joinings are a particularly important aspect of all of his work; the black screws and nuts and bolts delineate all the joints and connections. The dyed ash supports and runners and the triangular, anodized aluminum pieces contrast with the simple, linear aluminum form.

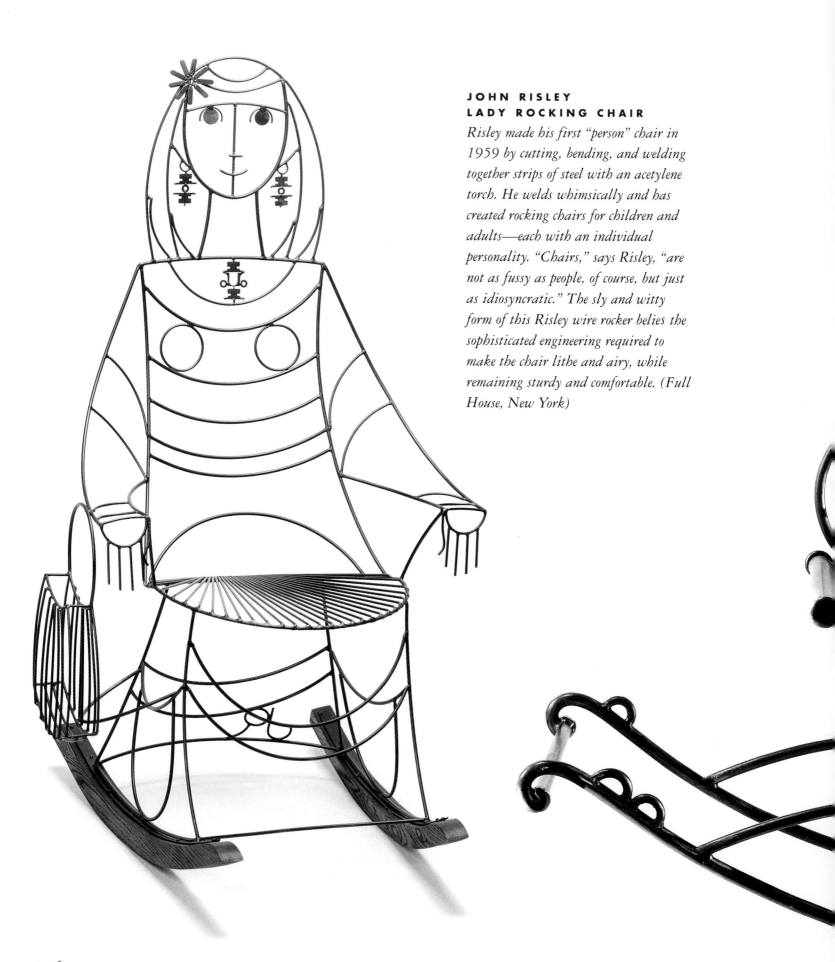

JOHN RISLEY
LADY ROCKING CHAIR

Risley made his first "person" chair in 1959 by cutting, bending, and welding together strips of steel with an acetylene torch. He welds whimsically and has created rocking chairs for children and adults—each with an individual personality. "Chairs," says Risley, "are not as fussy as people, of course, but just as idiosyncratic." The sly and witty form of this Risley wire rocker belies the sophisticated engineering required to make the chair lithe and airy, while remaining sturdy and comfortable. (Full House, New York)

**ILANA GOOR
ROSCOE ROCKING CHAIR**
*Ilana Goor is one of Israel's leading
artists who now shows her furniture
design in New York at the Decorator
and Design building. The inspiration
for her 1988 Roscoe award-winning
rocking chair was a child's sled.*

PHILIP MILLER
MUCH OBLIGED ROCKER
The artist chose the name for his rocking chair from a blues song sung by Taj Mahal: "You got a handful of gimmie and mouthful of much obliged." Miller's rocking chairs are incomplete without the heads of their users. (Gallery of Functional Art, Santa Monica, California, Matti Klatt)

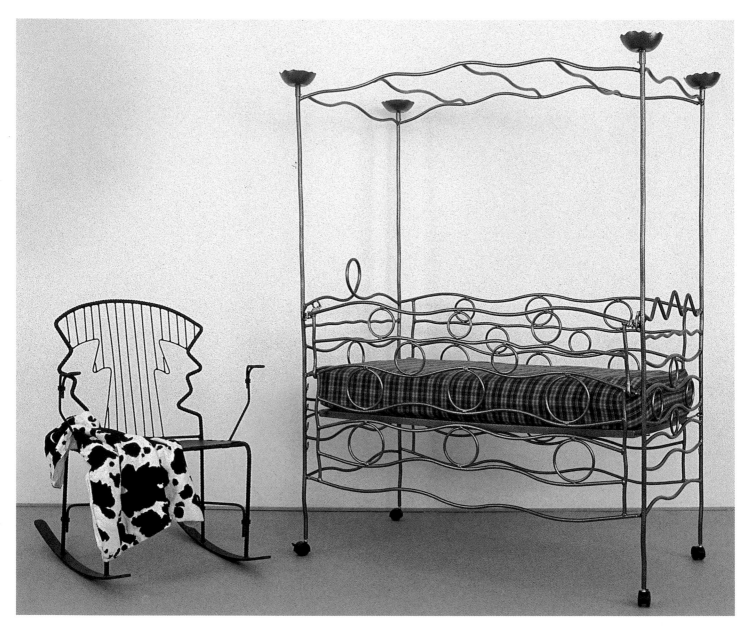

RIES NIEMI
HEAD ROCKING CHAIR AND CRIB

Niemi is a craftsman who makes functional objects and tries to imbue them with his spirit before sending them into the world. The artist reports that his two main inspirations are: "The first words uttered by the discoverer of king Tut's tomb, 'I see things; I see wonderful things'" and: "the photographs of the debris field around the Titanic—hundreds of manmade objects strewn about a landscape where men had never been. Timeless and mysterious, but enduring." (Gallery of Functional Art, Santa Monica, California)

FORREST MYERS
LA FARGE

In La Farge the user is enveloped in a bundle of black oxidized steel wires—hardly the comforting, nurturing associations one generally makes with a rocking chair. Like Calder, Myers uses simple wire to make magic. He approaches furniture design as an artist approaches a canvas. (Art et Industrie, New York, Joseph Coscia, Jr.)

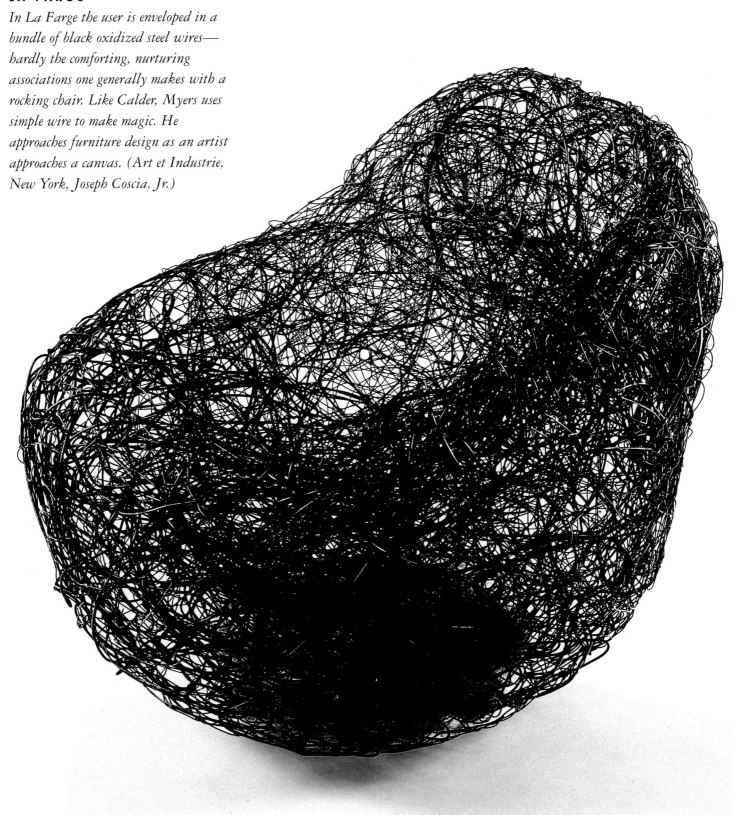

FORREST MYERS
SAIL AWAY

Forrest Myers, sculptor and furniture designer, is like many other artists who began designing furniture for their own use. Myers' work blurs the boundaries between fine art and furniture, between formal connoisseurship and active daily use. Sail Away rocks in two directions. The stainless steel chaise rocks side to side while the entire piece rocks lengthwise along the steel pipe. (Art et Industrie, New York, Joseph Coscia, Jr.)

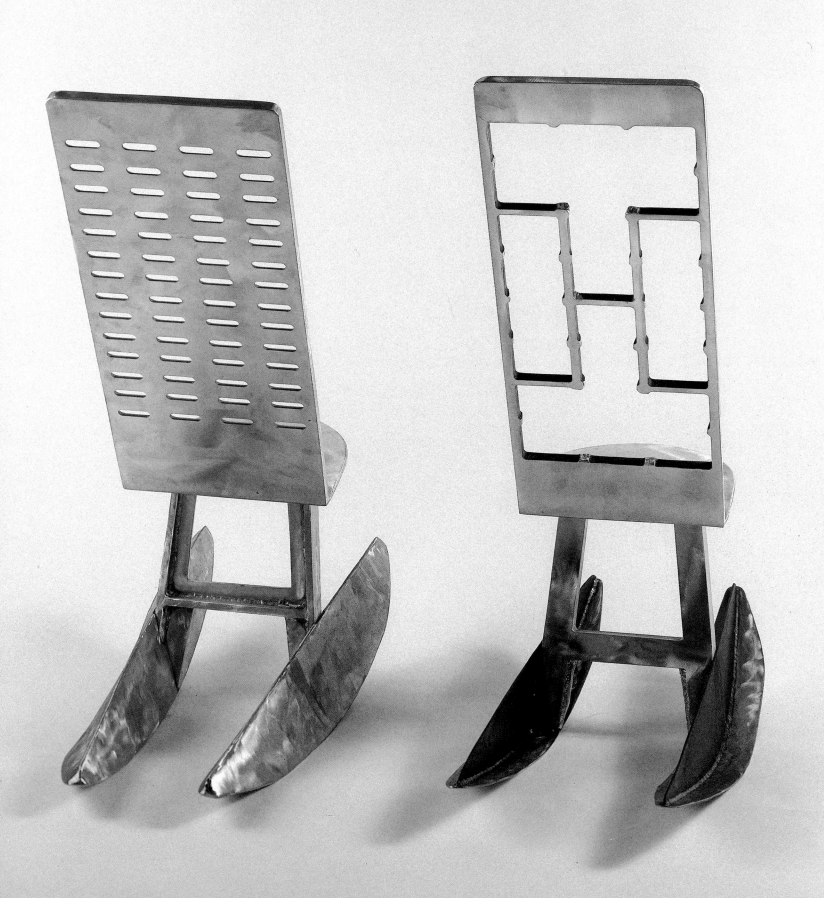

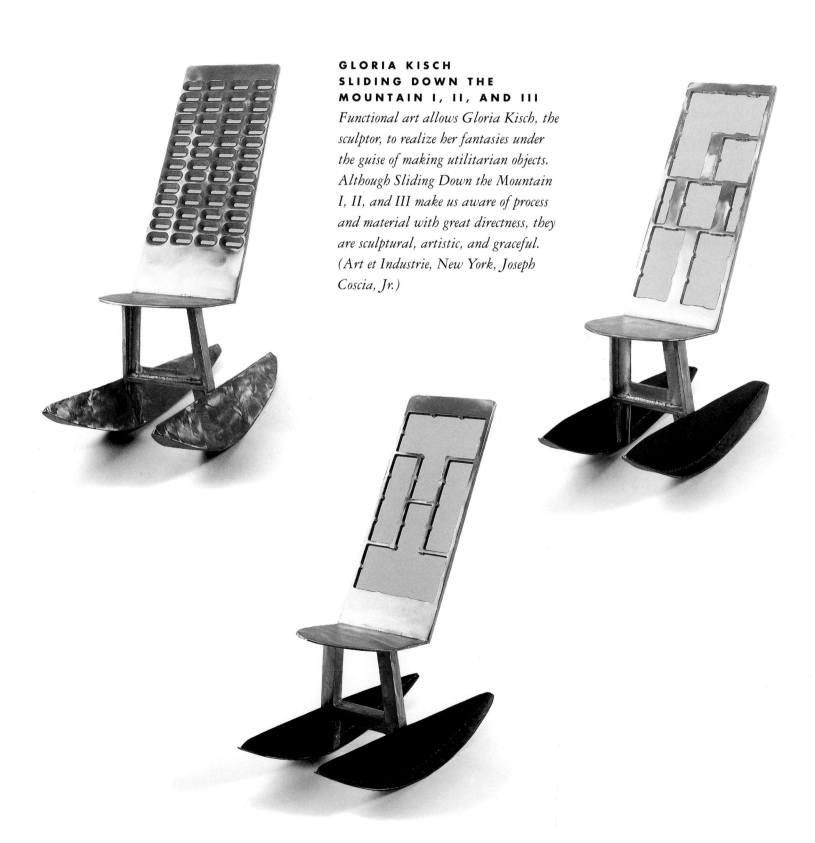

GLORIA KISCH
SLIDING DOWN THE
MOUNTAIN I, II, AND III

Functional art allows Gloria Kisch, the sculptor, to realize her fantasies under the guise of making utilitarian objects. Although Sliding Down the Mountain I, II, and III make us aware of process and material with great directness, they are sculptural, artistic, and graceful. (Art et Industrie, New York, Joseph Coscia, Jr.)

RON AMES
SANTA FE ROCKING CHAIR

Ames pays homage to the great American western landscape. The artist was inspired by the terrain and colors he saw on a trip to Sedona, Arizona. What better way to ruminate about these natural wonders than in a rocking chair painted with the same intensity of spirit?

TRENT HICKMON
LET'S ROCK

Let's Rock is a whimsical expression of language. Each generation redefines the subjective nature of language. "Let's Rock" is a visual play on words. (Gallery of Functional Art, Santa Monica, California)

**HELENE BRANDT
TWO-SEATED ROCKING
DRUM**

*Brandt created a bicycle-parts series of
sculptures between 1977 and 1979. The
Two-Seated Rocking Drum requires two
players, seated back to back. They each
use two drumsticks to create music on
drums of Chinese woks and rawhide.
(Bernice Steinbaum Gallery, New York)*

**FOLLOWING:
MITCH RYERSON**

*These children's rockers by Mitch
Ryerson are an assemblage of objects
constructed of detergent box logos, wash
boards, and spindles made of clothespins.*

Non-functional Rockers

. . . But, the rocking chair need not always be functional; while it has inspired generations of furnituremakers to new design heights, it has also been an element in the work of many sculptors and painters. They would argue, however, that art is, indeed, functional.

JOSETTE URSO
STANLEY

This work is part of a group of rocking, tipping, swaying, and nodding projects. Urso takes the posture of a rocking chair and satisfies the artist's desire to merge figure with object.

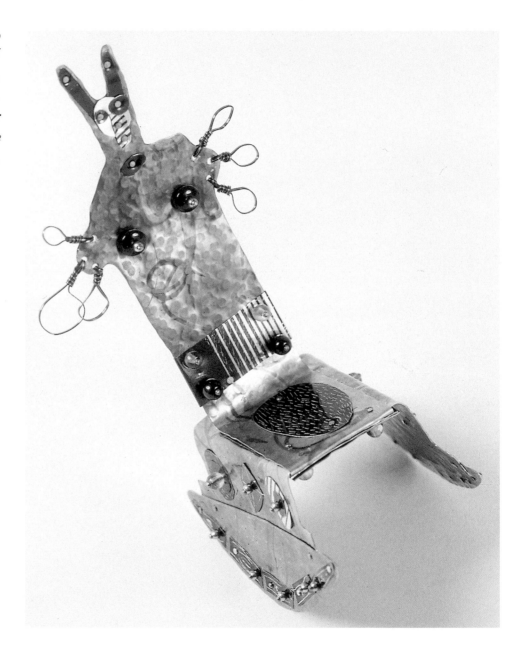

DAVID BEST
CHILDREN'S STUDY CHAIR

Best synthesizes the nostalgic and surreal with elements of his childhood into this gold-painted children's rocker. Even though the artist uses personal objects, they evoke memories of a universal childhood. (Shoshana Wayne Gallery, Santa Monica, California)

*Miller makes Afro-Deco furniture
pieces. The artist transforms metal porch
chairs by painting them with hot, spicy,
and tropical patterns in green, red,
yellow, and black. His work celebrates
clichéd images of blacks; he scatters his
furniture with motifs based on
watermelons, thick smiling lips, and
bright white teeth. In the past, blacks
reviled such images, but now they are
collecting this material and
participating in its analysis and
marketing.*

*The schematic rocking chair here almost
completely delineates the woman's body it
contains.*

WILL BARNET
EARLY MORNING

Barnet is a painter and printmaker whose images radiate elegance and serenity. In this work, the interior space, as well as the figure, are pared down to their essentials. A quiet intensity is created, which transports the viewer into an intimate setting.

GEORGE BELLOWS
ANNE IN WHITE

Bellows, the American realist who is best known for his street scenes, also painted many portraits and interiors. This portrait is of his daughter. (The Carnegie Museum of Art, Pittsburgh, Patrons Art Fund, 25.7, Richard Stoner)

EDWARD HOPPER
ROOM IN BROOKLYN
Hopper was one of America's great realist painters. Many of his paintings depict
isolated figures in rooms. He often used changing qualities of light to convey both the
time of day and the mood of a painting; this technique is clearly evident here. (The
Museum of Fine Arts, Boston, Charles Hayden Fund)

*This drawing on paper is a study for
Wyffels' sculptural rocker, The Poet,
illustrated on the following page.*

RON WYFFELS
THE POET

In his sculptural rocking chair, Wyffels contemplates the roundness of the world. Through the chair he implies that natural expansion and compression affect us not only individually but also influence a singular object.

**MARGARET WHARTON
HEIRLOOM**

Wharton's elongated "Heirloom" chair is made out of jointed flexible sticks. These segmented forms are too limp to stand on their own, so the chair dangles from the ceiling on wires like a marionette. (Phyllis Kind Gallery, New York)

*Buchanan celebrates her southern
heritage through her drawings,
sculptures, and photographs. Her three-
dimensional work is accompanied by
legends that she writes. Buchanan saved
this chair from the junk heap. It
originally belonged to R.A. Miller.
Buchanan embellished the chair and
wrote the following legend:
"R.A. Miller is a folk artist in north
Georgia. He said this half-buried chair
would make good firewood as he put it
in my truck. Mrs. Miller had decreed it
be used for firewood some time ago. The
Millers wouldn't recognize it and it
could still be firewood if Mrs. Miller
sees it. Don't tell her! She's a good shot."
(Bernice Steinbaum Gallery, New York)*

ISAMU NOGUCHI
APPALACHIAN SPRING
ROCKING CHAIR

*Noguchi's classical and elegant
sculptures are often focused on both
natural and manmade forms. In this
bronze sculpture, he employs his abstract
vocabulary in order to evoke a forceful
and beautiful rocking chair. (Marisa
Del Re Gallery, New York)*

ELIZABETH LAYTON
REMEMBERING AND
MOTHER'S DAY

Layton's drawings offer a view of American life rarely reflected in contemporary art. Aging, depression, dieting, marriage, grandmothering, death, Jonestown, world hunger, nuclear threat, capital punishment, and the ERA are all themes she has dealt with in her colored pencil drawings. Layton uses her own image—or that of her husband—in her art as a way of fusing the personal and political.

STEVEN TUCKER
HUSH LITTLE BABY

Steven Tucker's miniature assemblage was constructed by the intuitive selection of symbolic objects. The work layers symbols of past experiences. From the seat sprouts another even tinier red rocker that is attached to a metronome. When set in motion, the smaller chair ticks back and forth at a frenzied pace, suggesting an angry child.

(Marty Fumo)

Artschwager incorporates the mundane
industrial materials of formica and
plywood into a deadpan "High Art"
rocking chair. (Leo Castelli, New York)

FAIRFIELD PORTER
LOGS AND ROCKING CHAIRS AND THE CHRISTMAS TREE

Porter used traditional subjects of landscapes, still-lifes, and interiors to explore the play of light, color, and shape. Porter was primarily concerned with painting what lay before him. In these two works, the artist makes us aware of the magic we can discover in ordinary objects.(Private collection; Christmas Tree, photography by Eric Pollitzer)

59/100

Fairfield Porter

HELENE BRANDT
CRADLE

Cradle is part of a series of body enclosing sculptures that Brandt made between
1979 and 1989. It was made in the form of an adult curled up in a fetal position.
It can be opened up and a person can lie inside and rock back and forth.
(Bernice Steinbaum Gallery, New York)

NANCY WISSEMANN-WIDRIG

JUNE RAIN

When this artist bought a cottage on the coast of Maine with her family, the front porch was filled with rocking chairs belonging to generations of the home's former owners. These rockers suggested to the artist the people who had once rocked in them as they looked out to sea. (Tatitcheff Gallery, New York)

LISA DINHOFER
FUNHOUSE CORNER

Dinhofer's work forces the attention and imagination of the viewer to focus on the intricate details of objects one might otherwise pass by or discard. In this painting, the memories of a childhood are distilled through the reflections of the adult artist. The brightly painted marbles, a penny bank, and the dollhouse rocking chair are nostalgic symbols of youth.

BIBLIOGRAPHY

Ames, Kenneth, ed. *Victorian Furniture.*
Philadelphia: Victorian Society in America,
1983.

Andrews, E. D. and F. *Shaker Furniture: The
Craftsmanship of an American Communal
Sect.* New York: Dover Publications, 1964.

Applebome, Peter. "Winds of Change Rock a
Classic Rocking Chair," in *The New York
Times,* March 7, 1990.

Bowman, John S. *American Furniture.* New
York: Exeter Books, 1985.

Butler, Joseph T. *Field Guide to American
Antique Furniture.* New York: Facts on File,
1985.

Comstock, Helen. *American Furniture.* Exton,
Pennsylvania: Schiffer Publishing, Ltd., 1962.

Country Furniture. Alexandria, Virginia: Time-
Life Books, 1989.

*Eastlake-Influenced American Furniture:
1870–1890.* Yonkers, New York: The
Hudson River Museum, 1974.

Fairbanks, Jonathan, and Elizabeth Bidwell
Bates. *American Furniture: 1620 to the
Present.* New York: Richard Marek
Publishers, 1981.

Fales, Dean A. *American Painted Furniture
1660–1880.* New York: E.P. Dutton & Co.,
1972.

Fitzgerald, Oscar P. *Three Centuries of
American Furniture.* Englewood Cliffs, New
Jersey: Prentice Hall, 1982.

Gilborn, Craig. *Adirondack Furniture and the
Rustic Tradition.* New York: Harry N.
Abrams, 1987.

Hanks, David A. *Innovative Furniture in
America.* New York: Horizon Press, 1981.

Kassay, J. *The Book of Shaker Furniture.*
Amherst, Massachusetts: University of
Massachusetts Press, 1980.

Kovel, Ralph and Terry. *American Country
Furniture.* New York: Crown, 1965.

Madigan, Mary Jean and Susan Colgan, eds.
*Early American Furniture from Settlement to
City.* New York: Billboard Publications,
1983.

Muller, C. R., and T. D. Reiman. *The Shaker
Chair.* Columbus, Ohio: The Canal Press,
1984.

Ormsbee, Thomas H. *Early American
Furnituremakers.* New York: Tudor, 1930.

Pain, Howard. *The Heritage of Country
Furniture.* New York: Van Nostrand
Reinhold, Ltd., 1978.

Potter, P., and C. Anthea. "Sexual Division of
Labor in the Arts and Crafts Movement," in
Women's Art Journal: 1–6 (Winter 1985).

Rocker Shop of Marietta Georgia. *Georgia's
Brumby Heritage.* Marietta, Georgia: The
Rocker Shop, 1976.

Santore, Charles. *The Windsor Style in
America.* Philadelphia: Running Press, 1981.

Saunders, Richard. *Collecting & Restoring
Wicker Furniture.* New York: Crown, 1976.

Schwartz, Marvin D. *American Furniture of the
Colonial Period.* New York: Metropolitan
Museum of Art, 1976.

Smith, Mary Ann. *Gustav Stickley: The
Craftsman.* Syracuse, New York: Syracuse
University Press, 1983.

Smithsonian Institute Press for the Renwick
Gallery. *Shaker Furniture and Objects from
the Faith and Edward Deming Andrews
Collection.* Washington, D.C.: Smithsonian
Institute.

Sotheby's Concise Encyclopedia of Furniture.
New York: Harper & Row, 1989.

Stickley, Gustav. *Craftsman Homes.* New York:
Dover Publications, 1979.

OPPOSITE: *Maloof rocker in
Atlanta, Georgia.(Maria von
Matthiessen)*

INDEX

OPPOSITE: *A child's rocker in the shape of a cat. (Shelburne Museum, Shelburne Vermont, Ken Burris)*

ACKNOWLEDGMENTS

This book is the work and vision of many people. My collaborators were the historic rocking chair makers as well as the contemporary artists/furnituremakers, painters, sculptors, and photographers to whom I owe my deepest gratitude. Although some of your work is functional and others nonfunctional, all of you make magic that is often called art.

My literary agent, Carla Glasser, insisted that a book had to be written to prove my theory that the rocking chair was an American icon; further, she insisted that its writing was my responsibility. Who would deny a nine-months pregnant woman? Thank you for your staunch support and commitment to the rocker and this rocker.

My editor Sarah Burns' tenaciousness was as insistent as a toothache. Sarah, your editorial and technical contributions were invaluable. Your silences made a thunderous noise and your smiles made me soar. Do you agree, that in spite of our sparring, we can call it a draw? Sarah, you are the glue that holds this book together.

Robert Buganza, your research assistance was unparalleled. Carrie Steinbaum not only assisted with research, typing, and editing, but often exerted her four-foot-ten-and-three-quarter-inches height to physically make me complete the project. Carrie, I shall miss our private times together, but not your whips. Beth Tondreau had the impossible task of working graphically with an art dealer/author who probably had too much to say about the aesthetics, the layouts, the typeface, the margin size, the pica size, etc., etc., anon, of this book. You survived, Beth, congratulations! Applause to Nadine Gordon, artist par excellence, who made the illustrations that appear throughout this book, masterpieces.

Many others gave support, shared information and tolerated me during this tedious process of going "off and on my rocker." You know who you are—thank you for your patience and forgive me for not mentioning your names.

My special thanks too, to my family for their continuing support and encouragement.

Bernice Steinbaum

ABOVE: Naps *by Elizabeth Layton.*